Diener & Diener Architects
Housing

Diener & Diener Architects
Housing

Edited and with texts by Martin Steinmann,
Bruno Marchand, and Alexandre Aviolat, and
a conversation with Roger Diener

PARK BOOKS

Contents

	Preface	7
Bruno Marchand	Grids and Walls Some Thoughts on Diener & Diener's More Recent Façades	9
Alexandre Aviolat	Unstable Equilibrium A Typological and Morphological Study of Diener & Diener's Housing	19
Martin Steinmann	Marcus Diener Architekt Housing in Basel after World War II	31
	Housing—The Practice of Designing A Conversation with Roger Diener	45

Buildings and Projects 1978–2020

Hammerstrasse	Apartment Buildings, Basel	52
Riehenring	Apartment and Office Buildings, Basel	56
St. Alban-Tal	Apartment Buildings, Basel	62
Burgfelderplatz	Apartment Building with Bank, Basel	66
Allschwilerstrasse	Apartment Building, Basel	70
Bener Areal	Apartment Buildings, Chur	72
Hans Sachs Hof	Apartment Buildings, Salzburg-Lehen	74
Luzernerring	Apartment Buildings, Basel	80
Rue de la Roquette	Apartment Buildings, Paris	82
Warteckhof	Apartment Building, Basel	86
Hochbergerstrasse	Apartment Building, Basel	92
Parkkolonnaden	Apartment Buildings, Berlin	94
KNSM and Java-Island	Apartment Buildings, Amsterdam	98
Schönaustrasse	Apartment Building, Basel	104
Elsässerstrasse	Apartment Building, Basel	106
Ypenburg	Apartment Buildings, The Hague	108
Renaissance	Hotel and Apartment Tower, Zurich	112
Maaghof West	Apartment Building, Zurich	118
Casa A1, Olympic Village	Apartment Building, Turin	124
Westkaai	Apartment Towers, Antwerp	126
Île Seguin	Apartment Building, Boulogne-Billancourt	132
Schönwil	Apartment Buildings, Meggen	136
Markthalle	Apartment Tower, Basel	140
Favrehof	Apartment Building, Wallisellen	144
Via Suot Chesas	Apartment Buildings, Champfèr	150
GreenCity	Apartment Buildings, Zurich	152
Hardhof	Apartment Buildings, Bülach	156
Prannerstrasse	Apartment Building, Munich	162
Esplanade François Mitterrand	Apartment and Office Building, Lyon	164
Weidmatt	Apartment Buildings, Lausen and Liestal	166
Biographies		173
Image Credits		175

Preface

This publication collects buildings and projects that trace the involvement of Diener & Diener with housing construction over a period of more than forty years. The focus is primarily on the development of the thinking that becomes tangible in the various projects. While at least initially, the designs attempted to take the measure of the field of housing and its possibilities in terms of building and spatial structure, they gradually became consolidated into a repertoire of types that could be actualized according to the requirements of the specific commission. These requirements are economic and technical in nature, but also include the habits that prevail within a specific social context. The work of the Basel architects thus proves to be firmly anchored in the history of housing construction, and in a thinking that was never invalidated by the reforms of the early twentieth century, with their investigations into the scientific management of dwelling.

This constancy distinguishes the production of Diener & Diener when compared to architects who have experimented with "very different" forms of dwelling. This is not however to question the value of other architects' work (nor does Roger Diener do so), provided it is the expression of new ways of living. This corresponds to his profound sense of responsibility toward the people who live in his dwellings; and this same sense of social responsibility defines his architectural work in general.

Diener & Diener Architects has been the name of the office since 1980. A few years earlier, Roger Diener joined the architectural practice of his father Marcus Diener, becoming a partner when he was thirty years old. He assumed design responsibilities dealt with previously by employed architects. In 1978, the office received considerable attention for its first major project, in Basel's Matthäusquartier, which became known as the Hammerstrasse development. The project resolutely inscribed itself in the the ongoing debate on the "architecture of the city" both morphologically and typologically, and represents the the beginning of the office's research in the field of residential building.

While working on the present publication, it quickly became clear that Diener & Diener's housing construction has a prehistory that had to be mentioned, namely the work of Marcus Diener Architekt. Immediately after the war, the practice—founded in 1942—began building in Basel on a grand scale, initially for housing cooperatives at the edge of the city, then increasingly in the city center for building consortia founded by Marcus Diener with partners from the construction sector. Typologically, the buildings follow the development of residential construction in German-speaking Switzerland. There are barely any "inventions," perhaps with the exception of the apartment building. And here too, the architecture seems familiar: it ranges from the moderate modernism of housing estates from the 1940s to the "second modernism" of large-scale developments in the 1960s. The residential building of Marcus Diener, encompassing thousands of units, is discussed here in an essay by Martin Steinmann.

Two contributions address the development of housing construction by Diener & Diener since the Hammerstrasse project. Bruno Marchand investigates the look of the "houses" (as Roger Diener refers to his buildings), specifically the structural and formal resources—and their reciprocal interdependency—used in designing the facades. This encompasses the relationship between interior and exterior, which is controlled by these. Alexandre Aviolat explores the development of the floor plans. He brings out three or four types and shows how these are varied under the conditions of a given commission. These encompass the urbanistic situation of a particular site. This section concludes with a conversation between the editors and Roger Diener about the practice of housing construction. His statements summarize some of the fundamental insights that guide his work.

Part Two features thirty projects, each presented together with its urban planning situation and a brief description of the design and a standard floor plan, along with photographs. To facilitate comparisons, the plans have been redrawn: each is presented on a scale of 1:360. These examples do not however cover the entire residential work of Diener & Diener. We have restricted ourselves to multifamily dwellings, most of them realized. Among the works of these Basel architects, needless to say, are many designs that have remained on paper, i.e. competition entries. Because their plans are developed further en route toward realization, we have decided—with a few significant exceptions—to exclude unrealized projects from this book.

This book is based on material from the archive of Diener & Diener, little of which has been published. For the selection of plans and photographs, we were given unrestricted access to this extensive inventory. For a heightened understanding of the architectural thinking that is concretized in the residential building of Diener & Diener, we were able to conduct long discussions with Roger Diener. Moreover, we were allowed to view the typescripts of lectures in his personal archive. We are in his debt for the various forms of support we received for this project. This includes his collaborators, who assembled the necessary documents. Thanks as well to Park Books and its director Thomas Kramer, who encouraged our work on the book, to Anne Hofmann and Jörg Schwertfeger for its design and to Monique Zumbrunn for her careful editing.

Martin Steinmann, Bruno Marchand,
and Alexandre Aviolat

KNSM and Java-Island, Amsterdam, 1995–2001

Grids and Walls
Some Thoughts on Diener & Diener's
More Recent Façades

Bruno Marchand

In 1914 the art critic Adolf Behne noted that Bruno Taut had confined the expression of his designs to just two fundamental elements of architecture: "the wall and the opening."[1] He saw in this a way of saying that these elements should be sized and shaped mainly with a view to meeting the need for bright, functional spaces. He was opposed to an architecture bound by historical styles and wanted to emancipate it from the dead weight of history.

Were it not for the fact that his primary concern was to defend Expressionism, these same words might be used to describe the kind of architecture that is characteristic of Diener & Diener. It is an architecture that is so much a part of our everyday lives that it looks as if it had always been there. The ordinary and deliberately banal expression of some of their residential buildings of the 1980s and 1990s no longer has to be proven.[2] As Roger Diener himself says: "The best case would be a façade that looks so much a matter of course that ultimately it belongs as much to the city as to the building."[3]

Let us dwell briefly on this question, a question that dominated discussion of Diener & Diener's architecture at a time when it was understood as "an architecture for the city."[4] From this perspective, the design of the window rests on the familiarity that it arouses. This approach entails concentrating on the constituent elements of the window: the frame, the fixed and moving window leaves, the shutters, the window ledges, and so on and so forth. The window of the Warteckhof (1992–1996) in Basel is an emblematic example of this; its expression is that of a large hole in the wall that is defined by a flat reveal and by the difference between fixed and moving window leaves.

This expressive minimalism reduces the opening to its essentials without any recognizable rhetoric. It ascribes equal importance to the perception of the window from both inside and out. The ambivalence lies in the conception of the window, which according to Roger Diener references a general, collective image of a façade on the one hand and its specific, individual perception on the other.

"Familiarity" is associated with another quality, too, that of "singularity." The Warteckhof achieves the latter quality by accentuating the dimensions and the proportions of the openings. The windows here, being of an unusual shape and size, really do reveal "something else," and that "something else" prevents things from becoming locked into any one definitive meaning. This singularity is fundamental; it preserves the essential characteristics of the window, making it instantly recognizable even as it thwarts any all too obvious interpretation. In other words, it induces us to "imagine the obvious."[5]

Let us also mention "repetition" as a third quality that is as ordinary as it is artistic and that implies that "the appearance of the façades is defined by the regular spacing of identical windows."[6] Following the Smithsons, this would mean that the repeated elements ensue from the "whole to which they belong" and that they "derive their meaning from their own repetition." This has the effect of weakening the singularity of the elements for the sake of the uniformity of the whole,[7] as is especially apparent in the two residential buildings on the Rue de la Roquette (1992–1996) in Paris, where the façades, with their limestone cladding, are perforated by regularly spaced windows that lend them a "timeless character."[8]

Other, critical shores?

"Familiarity", "singularity", "repetition"—the attention paid to the window turns out to be central to the delineation of these concepts. Although the theme of the window in Diener & Diener's architecture has been discussed more than once before, questioning the possibility (and pertinence) of any new interpretation is entirely legitimate.[9] Why pace out a plot that others have already plowed only to reach the same conclusions as they did? The more reasonable approach would be "put the pencil down" in the belief that there is nothing to be added to what others have already thought and written, at least not without distorting it.

Yet I am still going to risk returning to this theme and viewing it in a broader framework, specifically that of architectural expression per se, in order to gain a surer grasp of the questions I have been asking myself. My hypothesis is that there are other ways of composing façades to be found in Diener & Diener's architecture, and that at least some of these mark a departure from the dominant discourse on the window as a *trou dans le mur*—a hole in the wall. Their more recent housing

---

1. Adolf Behne, "Ein neues Haus!" in *März 8*, no. 1 (1914), pp. 32–33, p. 33.
2. See Martin Steinmann, "Le sens du banal," in *Faces*, no. 13, autumn (1989), pp. 6–11; and Wilfried Wang, "From Normality to Abstraction: Diener & Diener's Recent Works," in *From City to Detail. Selected Buildings and Projects by Diener & Diener Architekten*, Berlin/London 1992, pp. 34–43.
3. Roger Diener, "Firmitas," lecture at the ETHZ, October 1996, published in *Diener & Diener*, London 2011, pp. 157–165.
4. Martin Steinmann, "L'architecture de Diener & Diener—une architecture pour la ville," in *Faces*, no. 41, summer (1997), pp. 2–3.
5. Here I have borrowed the title of the book by Álvaro Siza, *Imaginer l'évidence*, Marseille 2012.
6. Roger Diener, "Zum Entwurfsprozess und zu den verwendeten Mitteln," in *Die Wohnung im Fenster / Fenêtres habitées*, catalog of the exhibition at the Architekturmuseum Basel, Basel 1989, pp. 32–49, p. 41.
7. "The elements repeated seem to derive from the intention of the whole of which they form the part, the elements seem to gain their meaning only in repetition, i.e. were not pre-conceived or designed in the abstract as one and the repeated." Alison and Peter Smithson, in *Without Rhetoric*, London 1973, p. 30.
8. Joseph Abram, "Un caractère intemporal. A propos de l'immeuble de la Roquette à Paris," in *Faces*, no. 41, summer (1997), pp. 20–21.
9. See Martin Steinmann, "Die allgemeinste Form—Zur Entwicklung des Werks von Diener & Diener," and Ulrike Jehle-Schulte Strathaus, "Der Blick durchs Fenster," in Ulrike Jehle-Schulte Strathaus and Martin Steinmann (eds.), *Diener & Diener*, Basel 1991, pp. 25–31 and 33–37; see also Martin Steinmann, "Le regard producteur. A propos de la maison du Kohlenberg à Bâle," in *Faces*, no. 41, summer (1997), pp. 6–10, and Andreas Janser, "Das grosse Fenster," in *archithese*, no. 5 (1997), pp. 28–33.

St. Alban-Tal, Basel, 1984–1986

projects certainly reveal other concerns that must be identified if we are to understand the trajectory of their architectural language. These questions will guide me on my journey through time, the course of which is staked out by milestones both written and built, all of which attest to a development that is neither unambiguous nor unidirectional.

Compactness

Before discussing the recent characteristics of Diener & Diener's architectural language, let us first note one of the recurring hallmarks of their works, namely their utilization of orthogonal, compact volumes without any projecting or cantilevered parts. Any "extensions" of the apartments they contain therefore have to take the form of through balconies or verandas. They therefore avoid the balconies that Quatremère de Quincy rejected so vehemently on the grounds that "nothing sets the order of palaces apart from that of houses quite as much as those protuberances that come across as the calling card of puerile boldness."[10]

Diener & Diener prefer "extensions" that are wholly within the built volume so that their expression scarcely stands out—if at all—and the façades are assured a flat and compact appearance. What this also exposes is a certain relationship to the street and to the public space generally. The "sedimentations" of daily life familiar to us from many balconies do not enter our field of vision, but remain at a distance, as if out of respect for the notion of urbanity. Does this stance also impact Diener & Diener's treatment of other parts of the façade?

On walls *versus* grids …

Speaking in Dortmund in 2006, Roger Diener mentioned two archetypal openings designed by Walter Gropius and Le Corbusier respectively: the tripartite, "autonomous" windows of the Bauhaus student dormitory (1925–1926) and the aluminum-framed glass walls of the Pavillon Suisse (1930–1932) in Paris.[11] Drawing on this illuminating comparison, one could of course discuss, as Diener did, the individual dimension of the first opening as opposed to the collective and egalitarian dimension of the second. But it seems to me important, if only to support what I am about to say, that they also be related to two constructive and aesthetic figures: the wall and the grid.

These two figures materialize, almost literally, in the small residential building with a bank on Burgfelderplatz (1982–1985) in Basel. It is known mainly for its front facing onto a busy street and hence is often compared with the Luckhardt's Telschow House in Berlin (1928).[12] But our concern here is with the other façades. For that facing the courtyard, Diener & Diener really did borrow those L-shaped windows from Dessau—with only two leaves, but with a balcony enclosed inside a "naval-style" metal railing. The front facing the side street, by contrast, is punctuated by windows that are almost square and divided by mullions and transoms into four leaves each.[13]

---

10 Quatremère de Quincy, *Dictionnaire historique d'architecture comprenant dans son plan les notions historiques, descriptives, archéologiques, biographiques, didactiques et pratiques de cet art*, vol. I, Paris 1832, p. 148.

11 Roger Diener, "Fenster," lecture in Dortmund, April 28, 2006, typescript, archive Roger Diener.

12 See Karl-Heinz Hüter, "Die Basler Wohnbauten," in *Diener & Diener*, (see note 9), pp. 9–17; Hüter also mentions the Petersdorff (1926–1927), a commercial building in Breslau by Erich Mendelsohn and the Telschow House (1928), likewise a commercial building in Berlin by Hans and Wassili Luckhardt and Adolf Anker, which is also mentioned in the text by Martin Steinmann in the same publication.

13 These windows show a stylistic continuity with the large, four-part windows of the Sudgen House (1955–1956) by Alison and Peter Smithson, the Vanna House (1962–1966) by Robert Venturi, and the apartment building by Aldo Rossi in the Gallaratese district of Milan (1967–1972).

Parkkolonnaden, Berlin, 1994–2000

These windows are large and evenly spaced, irrespective of how the rooms behind them are used, and almost form a grid.

The building thus responds to its larger urban context, and thanks to the architects' use of archetypal windows blends into it. This striving for an "expressive differentiation and connection of fragments" continues in the St. Alban-Tal development (1981–1986) in a part of Basel close to the Rhine whose artisanal character dates back to the Middle Ages.[14] Despite their affinity, these early works—two residential buildings straddling an industrial canal—each have a completely different architectural expression attesting to a postmodernist spirit.

Let us first take a closer look at the openings in the building that faces the Rhine. These are arranged in four horizontal rows kept in check by "classical" *tracés régulateurs.* The L-shaped windows from Dessau are part of this, but here have no balconies. The rendered and whitewashed façade stands out on account of its frontality and so reminds us of what Colin Rowe once said of certain buildings by Le Corbusier: that they looked as if "cut with a knife."[15]

Whereas the general composition abides by the traditional stacking of pedestal, corpus, and cornice, the rows of windows have two countercurrents with the lower and upper ones "flowing" to the right and the middle ones to the left. Following the principle that "the image of the window that goes back to 'archetypal' spatial orders must be connected in parallel with the image of the floor plan," they transfer the free flow of the "day spaces" to the outside.[16] They therefore provide a dynamic with which to counterbalance the equilibrium of the composition.

The figure of this façade is at once both static and dynamic. In contrast to this tense balance of forces, the façade of the second residential building that faces the canal is defined by a grid. This neutralizes the viewer's reading of its functions and in a certain sense recalls the site's industrial past. The aim really is to evoke not just the history of the district, but also, as I see it, the rationality of Le Corbusier, as manifested in the Pavillon Suisse's window front. The two buildings are engaged in a dialogue conducted via two different stylistic registers according to the logic of the floor plan and the construction. Roger Diener thus evokes a confrontation between "skeleton" and "free floor plan" and its expression in the façade—and ultimately the importance of context.[17]

. . . on walls *and* grids

As already said, Diener & Diener use two figures—the grid and the wall—in one and the same building, specifically that on Burgfelderplatz in Basel. They took a similar approach a few years later in the Parkkolonnaden (1994–2000) in Berlin, a development at the head of Giorgio Grassi's master plan. There, the two L-shaped volumes occupying the whole plot are separated by a narrow passageway leading into the courtyard that opens up to the south and is separated from the public space by a very beautiful, striated concrete wall with a fine coating of moss that is watered from time to time.

The sides facing onto both street and courtyard are again articulated as a homogeneous grid of posts and lintels made of red brick with almost identical dimensions. The infill, consisting of low walls made of the same material surmounted

---

14 Ulrike Jehle-Schulte Strathaus, "Komposition aus Fragmenten," in *archithese*, no. 1 (1986), pp. 13–18.
15 Colin Rowe, "The Provocative Façade: Frontality and Contrapposto," in Michael Raeburn and Victoria Wilson (eds.), *Le Corbusier—Architect of the Century*, London 1987, pp. 24–28.
16 Diener 1989, (see note 6), p. 38.

17 Roger Diener, lecture at the Departement d'architecture EPFL, November 16, 1986, typescript, archive Roger Diener; see Arthur Rüegg, "Konstruieren für einen Ort—Zu den Wohnhäusern im St. Alban-Tal Basel," in *From City to Detail* 1992, (see note 2), pp. 31–33. Rüegg draws a parallel between these two buildings and Le Corbusier's Citrohan and Domino models.

Casa A1 at the Olympic Village, Turin, 2003–2006

by large, two-leaf windows, is somewhat set back, while a strip of plate glass serves as parapet.

The grid in Berlin differs from that of the St. Alban-Tal building in Basel in that it is not *a priori* a direct reference to its larger context. Its adoption was rather born of the desire to assign all the rooms large openings, and in a homogeneous, neutral way that reveals nothing of the typological diversity on the inside. The verticality of the duplexes is thus not visible on the outside. While this can indeed be read as an expression of a constructive logic, as the architects themselves affirm,[18] I cannot help but think that it is actually an abstract image of the grid, as described by the art critic Rosalind Krauss: "Its lack of hierarchy [...] emphasizes not only its antireferential character, but—more importantly—its hostility to narrative."[19]

If, as Krauss argues, the grid is an antireferential figure with a deliberate and rational order, then these façades can be compared with the two end walls facing south. Built of the same red brick, they are completely smooth—as if cut with a knife—and have almost square, staggered windows. For Martin Steinmann, windows of this type create a complex order that "can be described with the concept of relational art," i.e. with the search for the forces, counterweights, and relationships between the elements that "productive seeing" uncovers.[20]

The search for the forces at work on the end walls in Berlin, however, concerns a different window layout. The windows here do not "flow," but are rather part of an alternating play of full and empty, present and absent, all within two vertical lines. It really does look as if certain windows are missing or have been walled up, as they were in the Melnikov House (1925–1927) in Moscow. The resulting figure is enigmatic; it is difficult to understand the underlying rules. It gives us the strange feeling we get from looking at something that is incomplete. But that need not result in a negative view of the "offending" façades as an idiosyncrasy that blurs our reading of the whole.

How do the windows behave in relation to the inside? The question is justified since we are dealing neither with a typological turn to the south—as in Le Corbusier's Unités d'habitation—nor with "free" spatial arrangements. Here, the floor plan is the same on all eight stories, so the position of the window must play a role with regard to how the rooms are perceived and used. But the point of this figure is certainly not confined to that alone. Its meaning is an aesthetic one and grows out of the dialogue—or should I rather say confrontation?—between two figures in the same building: between grid and wall. The compositional freedom of the end façades really does reinforce the image of them as slim, closed, walled-up areas, whereas the seemingly random play of openings lends them a vibrancy that contrasts with the regularity of all the other façades.

Another purpose of this "game of chance" was to avoid the "pitfall" of perfectly aligned windows that would have had the effect of cutting the façade in half. The idea is similar to that of the all-over in art—a figure which ensures the integrity of the whole area. The end façades form a whole which, although perforated by windows, does not assert any particular vertical order. Thus they reference what is essentially a painterly image.

This long digression on the Parkkolonnaden in Berlin leads me to wonder whether the language of this development, which rests on the relationship between two different façades, does not expose a method that is very general in nature? The grid and wall can be regarded as two basic figures, *figures types*, whose aesthetic possibilities allow them to be used for different contexts and tasks, just as Marcus Diener and Roger Diener

18 Diener & Diener, "Abitare in Potsdamer Platz, Berlino," in *AREA*, no. 68 (2003), pp. 57–61.
19 Rosalind Krauss, *The Originality of the Avant-Garde and Other Modernist Myths*, Cambridge, MA 1985. p. 158.
20 Steinmann 1997, (see note 9), p. 9.

Île Seguin, Boulogne-Billancourt, 2005–2009

Maaghof West, Zurich, 2002–2013

use window typologies, door typologies, and even floor plan typologies in their architecture, sometimes in wholly new constellations and in a variety of contexts.

That combinations of these two figures are to be found in other projects and other forms is revealing. Take, for example, the small apartment building on Friedhofstrasse (1990–1992) in Birsfelden, where "the varied arrangement of windows on each floor signifies the free subdivision of rooms inside, in contrast to the loggias' regular openings";[21] and then the design of a hotel (1992, with Gilles Barbey) in Monthey, where the façade facing the square is defined by large windows that "are offset on the various floors, while on the other façades, they are organized on a regular grid."[22]

We might also mention the red brick building with a courtyard on Java-Island (1995–2001) in Amsterdam, where two reticulated façades are bracketed between two that are perforated by staggered windows, allowing the long, parallel layers of the interior organization to shine through. The dialogue of the main façade of Casa A1 (2003–2006) of the Olympic Village of Turin is implemented in a different register, but with a similar stratification of space. There, however, the grid is cantilevered over a series of staggered windows both high and low, horizontal and vertical, "which thwart the perception of stacked stories and create an impression that is as unstable as it is dynamic."[23]

Regular-irregular, static-dynamic—these are the antithetical registers whose aesthetic scope the architects exploit. This way of composing façades echoes Roger Diener's assertion "that architecture can always be conceived of as a collection of elements; that these elements can be constantly used and reused in a wide range of ways; and that sooner or later, this collection will form the basis of a new convention."[24] Presumably what he had in mind was the temporal dimension of urban architecture and the urban-planning conventions that remain valid, despite their variations over time. But it is tempting to think that this same statement is also an expression of his own design method at the level of floor plans, architectural elements, and the composition of façades.

From railings and parapets …

Let us return for a moment to the comments made at the beginning of this text. It is interesting to note how Behne, when discussing Taut, named a third basic element of architecture that in his eyes was just as important as both wall and opening, namely "delight in decoration."[25] He therefore assigned a crucial role to an element, and its artistic dimension, that was banished from architecture at the transition to Neue Sachlichkeit.

The delight in decoration in Diener & Diener's housing projects manifests itself in their railings. Diener and Barbey

21 "Apartment building, Friedhofstrasse, Birsfelden," in *From City to Detail* 1992, (see note 2), p. 90.
22 "Hotel, Monthey," 1991, in *From City to Detail* 1992, (see note 2), p. 92.
23 "Diener & Diener Architekten, Villaggio Olimpico Torino 2006 Lotto 3 Casa 1," Basel, December 3, 2003, typescript, p. 1, archive Roger Diener.

24 Roger Diener in conversation with Martin Steinmann, March 14, 1997, quoted in Martin Steinmann, "Die Architektur von Diener & Diener— Eine Architektur für die Stadt, (see note 4), p. 3.
25 Behne 1914, (see note 1), p. 33.

Schönwil, Meggen, 2006–2012

acknowledged the aesthetic importance of wrought-iron railings in their "Fenêtres habitées" studio at the ETH Lausanne back in 1988, contrasting their fine scrollwork with the very plain openings in the walls of the Îlot du Tunnel in that city.[26] The large windows facing the courtyard of the Warteckhof in Basel, which are generally photographed from the inside, extend almost from floor to ceiling and have a low masonry parapet and railing consisting of three horizontal metal bars.

The attention given to this element has increased in Diener & Diener's more recent projects. One good example is their T-shaped apartment building (2005–2009) in Boulogne-Billancourt, which was part of an open block development designed in collaboration with Vogt Landschaftsarchitekten and the outcome of a 2005 competition, which they won. According to the architects, the development can be read "as a conventional perimeter block punctuated by the gaps between the buildings, or as a sequence of complex buildings that on the outside form a trapezoid and on the inside delimit different urban spaces, courtyards, and gardens."[27]

Both these readings are premised on the same conceptual intent: to weave together buildings, squares, and gardens. This weaving is not confined to the contrast between full and empty, however, but extends to the material level, too. For all their artistic dimension, the prefabricated concrete parapets designed by the artist Peter Suter in front of the windows and balconies seem to be a response to the leafy environs. Their vertical slits are staggered and widen slightly toward the middle. The flickering effect that this generates spreads over the whole façade, including the loggias, all the way up to the cornice. The effect contrasts with the front facing the square in the middle of the development, which is another flat surface animated by small windows, positioned seemingly at random.

Another building where we can observe this effect is the Maaghof West (2002–2013) in Zurich, a linear building that is part of a development planned by Roger Diener together with Martin and Elisabeth Boesch. Here the flickering emanates from the parapets of the loggias on the west side of the building and of the windows on the east. The openwork pattern is generated by offset round bricks made of concrete. Unlike the deliberately artful ornamentation in Boulogne-Billancourt, the simple, somewhat archaic pattern of the round bricks evokes the romantic mood of a villa by Schinkel or a little house in the suburbs. Thus the loggias become outdoor rooms that are at once airy and intimate. The underlying motivation may be very different, but it is impossible not to notice parallels with the political and social goals of Italian Neorealism and architects such as Ludovico Quaroni and Mario Ridolfi, who after the war injected just such vernacular patterns into districts like Tiburtino in Rome, believing that the workers flocking there from the countryside would be especially receptive to them.

Roger Diener himself has attributed these round brick parapets to just such a "yearning for the south."[28] In Zurich they cover the whole of the west façade where they are held in place by slender, load-bearing structure of reinforced concrete. Its intricacy softens the austere or even monotonous impression made by this exceptionally long building and makes it flicker. The architectural expression resulting from this is further enriched by a wide range of perceptions, arising in part from the treatment of the windows on the east side, which are fronted by the same kind of parapets. These are also staggered by one-brick-width per story, which is a motif that Diener & Diener used in Amsterdam, too. The casual observer has to look hard to spot this discreet measure, but it is certainly a factor in bringing the façade to life.

26 *Die Wohnung im Fenster* 1989, (see note 6), p. 65.
27 Diener & Diener Architekten, ZAC Seguin, Rive de Seine, Macro-lot A2, undated typescript, archive Diener & Diener.
28 Roger Diener in conversation the editors, November 21, 2018, in this book, p. 49.

Westkaai, Antwerp, 2005–2009

... to the mode of cladding

The Maaghof West project shows us Diener & Diener's architectural language absorbing decorative motifs and so affording us a certain visual pleasure, as it would later in Boulogne-Billancourt. Through the new materials and the feelings they arouse, these two buildings differ from the architects' other housing projects, most of which have concrete or brick walls with single, regularly spaced openings and are resolutely devoid of rhetoric.

The use of decorative elements has now spread, in part in response to the impact that new energy standards are having on the structural and architectural properties of contemporary buildings.[29] As Antoine Picon has noted, "the condition and performance of the structure are [now] often less important than the exchange of heat and light between inside and outside."[30] Roger Diener has always been committed to environmental questions in his own research, too.[31] Like many other architects, he has recognized the strategic importance of the façade as envelope and specifically its capacity to prevent heat losses from the cold bridges to which visible load-bearing structures on the outside of the building give rise. Cladding, in other words, is essential.

29 The oil crisis led to the inclusion of an energy clause in the Swiss constitution, which the electorate approved in 1991. It empowers the cantons to pass legislation aimed at lowering energy consumption in buildings.
30 Antoine Picon, *L'ornement architectural. Entre subjectivité et politique*, Lausanne 2016, p. 29 (original edition Chichester 2013).
31 Roger Diener in conversation with Winfried Nerdinger, Munich, July 3, 2004, typescript, archive Roger Diener.

To prove the point, let us return to the Maaghof. The expression here rests on the principle of dissociation through the use of a certain vocabulary that transcribes the layout of the spaces onto the façade. What has changed, however, is the quality of the outer cladding, which here consists of 25-cm-long facing bricks that are cemented vertically onto the thermal insulation. We should not be misled by appearances: these bricks are not load-bearing. They attest to a new, simple, and purposeful approach to building and to a "cladding principle" capable of complying with ever more exacting energy standards.

A similar spirit holds sway at Schönwil (2006–2012) in Meggen, which is another competition that Diener & Diener won. Here, two residential buildings on the fringes of a park enter into a dialogue with a manorial villa and the surrounding landscape. Slightly offset, they are obviously positioned to face the lake to the southeast. The floor plans make this clear: the stairwell situated next to the façade affords access to two or three apartments per story. The bedrooms are located at the rear, while the living rooms, enlarged by deep loggias, face the front.

Did the park with its big, old trees as the context of these buildings influence the choice of façade materials? Well, the architects' decision to use wood as cladding for the load-bearing structure made of concrete certainly followed Gottfried Semper's adage that "even where solid brick walls are necessary, these only ever form the inner structure hidden behind their true and legitimate representative: colored wallpaper."[32] The shell of standing gray boards in Meggen varies depending on the façade: On the sides of the building the boards form bands delineating the parapets of the loggias and the slightly set back windows, while at either end they cover the whole façade except for the three openings, one above the other. The overall impact is one of solidity, with the exception of the parapets, where the gaps in the shell once again produce a flickering effect.

The cladding and decoration of the residential buildings in Zurich and Meggen are an architectural theme developed in response to ever more exacting energy standards, but following a rational, technical, and economic logic. In this sense, we can certainly observe a continuity in the architects' thinking. The return to ornament in contemporary architecture is usually accompanied by "a weakening of the tectonic approach and by the growing importance attached to surfaces."[33] Yet curiously, the homogeneous cladding weakens neither the tectonic impact nor the impact of mass in either of these two projects by Diener & Diener.

The question of tectonics is raised by Diener & Diener's high-rises, too, specifically by the tower blocks Westkaai 1 and 2 (2005–2009) in the port of Antwerp and by the five-cornered Markthallen-Turm (2011) near the Swiss Railway Station in Basel. In both instances, Diener & Diener clad the façades first with aluminum panels covering the thermal insulation and then with panels made of ribbed glass, which lends these buildings an appearance whose color is constantly changing, depending on the prevailing light conditions.

"Diener & Diener's façades are generally structured so that the inner layer consists of load-bearing concrete, while the outer layer consists of a material that references the

32 Gottfried Semper, *Die vier Elemente der Baukunst. Ein Beitrag zur vergleichenden Baukunde*, Braunschweig 1851, p. 58.
33 Picon 2016, (see note 29), p. 29.

Favrehof, Wallisellen, 2008–2014

context."[34] In the case of the aforementioned high-rises, it could be said that they are bound to stand out from their surroundings and that thanks to the impact of the ribbed glass they also relate to a much wider built-up context. Perhaps "meteorological" and "playful" are the epithets that the sensation of lightness and airiness made by the towers' constantly changing façades first call to mind.

Interface and thick façades

The "cladding principle" has not, however, been adopted in other, more recent works by Diener & Diener that revisit the question of "construction en élévation."[35] In the course of a 1996 discussion of the Vitruvian concept of *firmitas*, Roger Diener reiterated his conviction that "the façade [is] not the image of the construction; it permits an exchange between the building and the city."[36] True enough, but even if the façade is not the image of the construction, its expression in many cases is the result of the choices made concerning its construction, or, to put it another way, of a constructive idea. In this sense, it is often a consequence of the construction.

We have seen how in Berlin the architects themselves insisted on the role of construction in their choice of a grid facing the street and courtyard. That same intent is evident in the Favrehof in Wallisellen (2008–2014), where the façades are structured by narrowly spaced pilasters. These invoke a constructive aesthetic and at the same time create an interface between the volume and the space that it delimits. The façades owe their thickness to their load-bearing function. The concrete pilasters are brightly rendered and create an architecture that takes up the monumental expression of the Stücki Hotel (2001–2009) in Basel. Their spacing is irregular, which has the effect of setting the façades "gently into motion"—to borrow Roger Diener's own turn of phrase.

Diener & Diener thus generate the impact of a heavy, deep façade. The pilasters on the street named Arkade seem to come adrift from the wall with the result that the façade splits open, becoming a space in its own right.[37] Sandwiched between the rooms delimited by the windows and window fronts and the façade with its pilasters made of rendered concrete are the loggias. Conceived as additional rooms, they are also interfaces in that they belong, paradoxically, to two worlds at once: the domestic and the urban. The same thing happens on the other three sides facing the courtyard. Their parapets are fluted in a way that dematerializes them and reinforces the structuring force of the pilasters. Interestingly, the architects apparently considered using round bricks here, too, at least initially. Their aim, however, was to find a clear urban expression, which is why they changed the design of the parapets.

The columns break free

Let us briefly dwell on this structural logic and how it translates into the expression of Diener & Diener's residential buildings, especially in relation to an element that is unusual for them: the column. As far as I know, their first round concrete columns were those used for the façade of the Maaghof, where they support the layer of projecting loggias on the west side of the building. On the ground floor, which is taller than the others, the columns are rectangular, but above that round.

Such columns also feature in a recently completed project—the three apartment blocks (Hardhof, 2012–2019)—

---

34 Martin Steinmann, "Die Gegenwärtigkeit der Dinge—Bemerkungen zur neueren Architektur in der Deutschen Schweiz," in Martin Steinmann, *Forme forte—Schriften 1972–2002*, edited by Jacques Lucan, Bruno Marchand, Basel 2003, p. 124.
35 Here I have borrowed the title of Chapter 11 in Eugène Viollet-le-Duc, *Histoire d'une maison* (1873), Gollion 2008, pp. 135–155.
36 Diener 1996, (see note 3), p. 161.

37 Michel Rémon, *La façade épaisse*, Paris 1978, p. 5.

Esplanade François Mitterrand, Lyon, 2016–2020

Hardhof, Bülach, 2013–2019

built on the site of a former foundry in Bülach as part of a new district, the master plan of which is also by Diener & Diener. Two of the buildings are positioned perpendicular to each other and are connected so that they shield the courtyard from noisy Schaffhauserstrasse. The third closes off the courtyard, which is planted with trees. Its projecting façade of thin slabs is supported by thick round columns. Set back from the front of the slabs, these form a layer of "open rooms" that extend the living rooms with curtains as dividers.

It is an engaging effect, further enhanced by the way the rounded ends of the balconies project slightly on either side. The enchanting appearance is all the more powerful on account of the façades opposite, which are structured by pilasters. Here, the architects again take up a motif first used in Wallisellen, but amplify the effect with floor-to-ceiling windows that give rise to a closely spaced sequence of full and empty, *des pleins et des vides*. The architecture seems austere, but thanks to the finely twisted bars of the railings it is also elegant.

Could these columns in Diener & Diener's architecture be an echo of those in other projects that fulfill other purposes, such as the columns made of brown-glazed concrete to make them look like cigars used for the Davidoff-Haus (2015–2017) in Basel? Since 2016 Diener & Diener, in association with Clément Vergély, have been building a high, orthogonal apartment block in Lyon's Confluence on Esplanade François Mitterrand district as part of a development around a large courtyard. Its aspirational qualities are clear from the colonnade that encircles the whole building and on the sides delimits the loggias. The prefabricated columns are each two stories high and in the courtyard especially lend the building an ambivalent impact—like the partitions between the loges of a civic theater, to quote Roger Diener himself.

For the architects, however, the colonnade "institutes a three-dimensional game that is visible from a distance and becomes stronger the closer one comes. The columns are asymmetrical in shape and are set in four different ways by being rotated on both the vertical and horizontal axes. This produces new outlines, which from a distance give an impression of 'interactive' tension. From close up the columns arouse even more powerful, physical, and spatial sensations, almost as if they were dancing."[38]

The continuous layer of 1.7-m-deep balconies on two sides lends the building permeability and finesse, without taking away from its compactness, which is a quality we spoke of earlier on. But it also shelters the façades, which are set back. The buildings' closeness to each other is attenuated by the railings, whose vertical bars, as in Bülach, twist upward in a way that opens up the parapets. Thus the inhabitants are assured of a certain intimacy without being deprived of natural light.

Reusing experience and other approaches

"In my view, the projects that are most important in terms of development are not necessarily those that were actually built.

[38] Diener & Diener Architekten, Clément Vergély Architectes, Ilot B2 Lyon-Confluence, presentation of October 30, 2015, p. 26; text by Christoph Joud, archive Diener & Diener.

What we learned from them was nevertheless of value to the projects that came after. We try to be creative every time, but without letting go of our experience. I like this domino effect—reusing something that you then combine with something new."[39]

As we can see, this "domino effect" is part of Diener & Diener's compositional tool kit. Through the basic figures of wall and grid, we have tried to show that this rational approach is very much in the spirit of a *recherche patiente*. The emergence of new, innovative connections would prove, as Le Corbusier claimed, that "the work of art is a game. You make up the rules of your own game,"[40] specifically those rules with which the player has to "compose," and whose mastery leads to the creative act itself.

This metaphor points out something else, too: the game of critical analysis of the object, since "you have to be able to dissect a building just as you dissect a game of patience to dispel any illusion regarding the position and function of each of its parts."[41] What is the role of ornaments in this game? Or that hint of monumentality that allows you to use solid pillars or sculpted columns, whose expression paradoxically approximates that of other programs such as offices?

Roger Diener remains attentive to the details—to the habits and practices that form the mosaic of daily life for inhabitants. But through his openwork parapets made of round bricks drawn from other worlds—from the romantic mood of nineteenth-century country estates, suburban gardens, or the festive, sunny terraces of the Mediterranean—he is now giving the expression of these practices a new, allegorical dimension.

With structure as a lever of monumentality, however, it must also be noted that Diener & Diener are now moving away from the ordinary and the deliberately banal and away from the idea that at first glance it is difficult to tell the difference between their housing and traditional developments. Now they arouse all sorts of contradictory feelings—among them surprise and familiarity: surprise at the more recent manifestations of an architectural language that sets itself apart from the register of the "ordinary" to which Diener & Diener's architecture has accustomed us, and familiarity, too, since all these projects belong to the same register of mass and force striving for that eye-catching unity that is a fundamental quality of their work; familiarity, since we experience the vibrancy that distinguishes so many of their designs, even in the sculpted columns of Lyon; and familiarity, finally, since the designs, for all the stylistic changes they have undergone, all share the same rationalistic approach. It is an approach that articulates the three levels of design: the ordering of the floor plan, the construction, and the incorporation of ornament as three conceptual levels that are indissolubly linked.

---

39 Roger Diener, untitled and undated typescript, archive Roger Diener.
40 Le Corbusier, "Vues sur l'art—Choix de citations par André Wogenscky," in *Revue d'esthétique*, vol. 1, Paris 1948, pp. 20–24, p. 21. English translation by John Tittenso quoted from *Le Corbusier—The Drawing Game*, catalog for the exhibition at Musée Picasso, Antibes 2015, n. pag.
41 Eugène Viollet-le-Duc, *Entretiens sur l'architecture*, vol. 2, Paris 1863–1872, p. 34.

Unstable Equilibrium
A Typological and Morphological Study of Diener & Diener's Housing

Alexandre Aviolat

No analysis of contemporary housing in Switzerland would be complete without a discussion of the architecture of Diener & Diener. Their work raises the question of the close and complex relationship between architecture and city. Far from offering a single, clear answer to that question, it creates scope for a sensitive, often intuitive, interpretation that can be read as a particular way of transforming the city through new relationships and, by doing so, changing our view of it.

Many texts describe Diener & Diener's architecture as an "architecture for the city," which on grounds of its architectural expression looks deliberately ordinary.[1] Yet rarely is any attempt made to explain it on the basis of its floor plans and its relationship to the city.[2] This also holds true for the relationship between inside and out, an important medium of which are the windows that render it visible.[3] It therefore seems appropriate to posit some hypotheses about how residential floor plans and city are correlated, and, even more crucially, to attempt to determine the nature of those correlations.

Design by typology

As much as we are bound by the typomorphological research done in Italy from the 1960s onward, we are of the opinion that Diener & Diener combine this heritage with concerns that are not directly related to the specific context.[4] Their way of working forces them to address the reconciliation of two fundamentally antithetical kinds of design. The first of these, following the logic of continuity in urban planning, postulates that a project must maintain a strong bond to the city, while the second, following the logic of rationalism, seeks suitable floor plans that can be used in a wide range of contexts. But how can we extrapolate from this an approach to each specific case that is premised at once on a site-specific stance and on a universally valid, typological order?

Without returning to the debates over what the concept of typology actually means, we can confidently assert that, to our mind, the floor plans in Diener & Diener's housing rest on just a few typologies that are then concretized from case to case.[5] Their approach is not new, since housing in general was for a long time characterized by the repetition of typologies, which besides answering the needs of specific social classes were shaped by the prevailing economic conditions and material possibilities.[6] In the case of Diener & Diener, this approach to design manifests itself as an inflection of typologies that are selected on grounds of certain features and then concretized in floor plans adapted to the conditions specific to the task in hand.

We can try to understand this approach as a variant of Neues Bauen. Roger Diener has explicitly said as much: "Certain methods repeat themselves in such design processes. They are part of the ongoing research. To the extent that they are typological in nature, they are based—at least in part—on the rationalistic exploration of these categories repeatedly undertaken ever since the 1920s."[7] Not only does Roger Diener acknowledge Diener & Diener's application of the same methods, but he also confirms the link between their practice and the typological quest defined during the interwar period. Appealing to this means above all following the clear distinction drawn by Adolf Behne between the two currents of the age: rationalism and functionalism.[8]

Rationalism

That Roger Diener has distanced himself from a concept in which every function has its own space and has instead moved closer to the approach taken by the rationalists is hardly surprising, since it was the latter who set out to find what Behne called "the best possible fit for general requirements—the norm."[9] This remains very much the stance of Diener & Diener, and it extends even to demanding the norm as a pledge of spatial neutrality.

One of the first consequences of rationalism is the almost systematic use of the right angle.[10] This question would have been familiar to Behne, who saw it as confirmation that the whole takes precedence over the parts. The right angle is apparent at all levels in the works of Diener & Diener, too. The "orthogonal room," explains Roger Diener, "is a sure basis for the organization of space. That is a consensus that can be traced a long way back into the history of human settlement."[11]

---

1   See Martin Steinmann, "Eine Architektur für die Stadt—Das Werk von Diener & Diener," in Martin Steinmann, *Forme forte—Écrits / Schriften 1972–2002*, edited by Jacques Lucan, Bruno Marchand, Basel 2003, pp. 59–63.
2   As far as the urban development form is concerned, see the classification used by Vittorio Magnago Lampugnani in "Tanzfiguren, fest gemauert—Anmerkungen zum Städtebau von Diener & Diener," in *Stadtansichten Diener & Diener*, catalog of the exhibition at ETH Zurich 1998, pp. 8–38.
3   The theme of windows in the works of Diener & Diener has been extensively discussed: see essay by Bruno Marchand in this book, pp. 9–18, in particular note 9 for sources; for illustrations see *Stadtansichten Diener & Diener* 1998, (see note 2), pp. 52–87.
4   We are thinking in particular of Saverio Muratori's research into the relationship between the typology of the building and morphology of the city, as e.g. Saverio Muratori, *Studi per una operante storia urbana di Venezia*, Roma 1960.
5   Among those in France to address the subject of typology was Bernard Huet, whose *L'Architecture d'aujourd'hui*, no. 5 of 1986, titled "Recherche Habitat," contains a very sound definition of typology in Christian Devillers, "Typologie de l'habitat et morphologie urbaine," pp. 18–23.
6   Consider, for example, Haussmann's Paris, whose housing rests on clear typologies, as explained in César Daly, *L'architecture privée au XIX siècle sous Napoléon III. Nouvelles maisons de Paris et des environs*, vol. 2 *Maisons à loyer*, Paris 1870.
7   Roger Diener, lecture script for a summer academy in Karlsruhe, 1990, typescript, archive Roger Diener.
8   Adolf Behne, *Der moderne Zweckbau*, Munich 1926, esp. pp. 62–63.
9   Behne 1926, (see note 8), p. 63.
10 Only a few residential high-rises by Diener & Diener diverge from this. These generally have a pentagonal footprint—the Markthallenturm in Basel, for example.
11 Roger Diener, "Einfache Ordnungen. Ästhetik der Reduktion anstelle eines formalen Chaos," lecture, April 1985, symposium at Technische Universität Dresden, typescript, archive Roger Diener.

The right angle thus shapes the rooms of his dwellings, assuring them of both a rational organization and an expression of the habitual. But what led Diener & Diener to the right angle was not their identification with a bygone movement, but rather the idea that it is space that shapes our perception of a dwelling.

A second consequence of rationalism is the systematic use of closed spaces, that is to say of rooms inside an apartment, as opposed to the striving for fluid, open spaces. Floor plans thus evolve as an agglomeration of rooms, and not—to use the expression that Le Corbusier was so fond of—as a *promenade architecturale*. It follows that the actual task of designing a dwelling consists in piecing together rooms much as one would a puzzle; in other words, each piece has to fit the others exactly in order to form a whole.

Not only is the use of rooms following the model of the residential developments of the 1920s somewhat rare in Switzerland, at least where the aim is to build on the legacy of Neues Bauen, but Diener & Diener's works also mark a departure from the tendency of so much contemporary architecture to simply multiply floor plans on the grounds that it is allegedly no longer possible to design dwellings that adapt to different habits.[12] And that is precisely the issue for floor plans consisting of just a few ordinary, often unspecific, spaces. The room remains a room and is familiar as such, even if it is rich in terms of the relationships it can enter into—both on the inside with other rooms and on the outside with the city. This approach is a common thread in all Diener & Diener's projects, irrespective of scale, and we shall return to it in due course.

Convention and use

Accepting that Diener & Diener's design work is stimulated by the rationalistic methods of the 1920s, it can also be said to enrich them through the more complex relationship between form and the use that it proposes.

We have seen how a special relationship to use is intrinsic to Diener & Diener's architecture and how that architecture is part of their investigation of the relationship between housing—housing typologies—and the city. "Our work on our projects has taken us beyond the rationalistic approach of the typological inquiry to the conscious perception and appropriation of still more characteristics of place for the design," Roger Diener explains. "These allow us to lend concrete form to a given typology, here defined as the sum of the conventions that are closely bound up with social structures, models, and constructive systems, as an architecture for a specific place."[13] Although Roger Diener here insists on the special relationship that he wishes to create between building and city, we also see him endeavoring to overcome any all too simple, rationalistic approach. But what does he mean by "sum of the conventions" and how, exactly, are those bound up with what he calls "social structures"?

Roger Diener undoubtedly cultivates the art of probing the conventions that we typically associate with our abode. "The inner organization of the dwelling need not determine human behavior," he writes, "although typically it will have been shaped by the constant repetition of domestic habits."[14] It is this repetition of habits that defines the conventions and hence, also, the typology. Habits, however, are not prone to abrupt change as a rule, but tend to develop organically. It is this "historical sedimentation of functions" that provides the substrate that enables a given typology to thrive.[15] Ultimately, therefore, a typology is the spatialization of all these layers in architecture.

So what is the putative connection between typologies and social structures? The "sum of the conventions" does not relate to individual people. It should rather be understood in the sense of Behne's assertion that what is crucial is the relationship to society![16] In his rationalistic view, the many take precedence over the individual. For Roger Diener, too, the relationship to society is essential to architecture and the dwelling an opportunity to affirm this relationship. "Housing, as the architecture of urban renewal," he explains, "holds out the prospect of putting our actions back in a larger context with society."[17] At the same time, he takes a more critical stance inasmuch as he does not view society as the sum of its parts, i.e. individuals, but rather as a whole that is defined by its habits and conventions. So we could say that his architecture seeks to be egalitarian as it attaches greater weight to conventions than to the needs of the few; and because it jettisons what is special, its de facto inclination is toward ordinariness.

Before addressing the subject of "ordinariness" in the work of Diener & Diener, we should first take a closer look at one particular matter relating to use. We do not regard a project merely as the outcome of conventions in which form and function are bound together in a simple causal relationship, since the relationship in question is not mechanical, but rather creative. There is a subjective dimension to every project and that dimension is tied to the decisions of the architects and enriches the said relationship. Roger Diener expresses this idea as follows: "In our design work we do not seek to model space according to its function, according to its 'use.' The approach to typology that we cultivate actually modifies the reciprocity between form and use that shaped Modernist architecture."[18] Ultimately, what is spatialized through the typology is the way Diener & Diener view conventions.

The point of things

"In general, we as architects try to express ourselves simply, and this applies to more than just the semiotic properties of our buildings," Roger Diener explains. "The disposition of space is also integral to the typologically oriented approach, from which we hope to achieve intelligibility. Hence there are very few inventions. We often repeat familiar floor plans and sometimes there are similarities with everyday, anonymous architecture."[19] Many authors have remarked on the unassuming look of Diener & Diener's façades and hence on the way they blend in with

---

12 A better reference from the early twentieth century would be the dissolution of space in the open-plan layouts of Le Corbusier and Mies van der Rohe. The return to rooms, by contrast, often harks back to the middle-class homes of the nineteenth century, especially in Haussmann's Paris.
13 Roger Diener, "Vortrag 3. Wiener Architekturseminar," lecture, Vienna, September 1992, typescript, archive Roger Diener.
14 Roger Diener, "Architektur im Dialog von Gestalt und Nutzung," lecture, Uni Basel, December 1992, typescript, archive Roger Diener.
15 Vittorio Magnago Lampugnani, *Die Modernität des Dauerhaften—Essays zu Stadt, Architektur und Design*, Berlin 2011, p. 99 (original edition 1999).
16 Behne 1926, (see note 8), p. 52.
17 Diener 1990, (see note 7).
18 Diener December 1992, (see note 14).
19 Diener September 1992, (see note 13).

Warteckhof, Basel, 1992–1996

the city.[20] But that is not all. The architects have allowed this sense of the ordinary to inform even our spatial perception of the floor plan. Here, we again see how repetition of a type allows the floor plan to be neutralized. By means of repetition, Diener & Diener resist all forms of invention as the production of ever new things.

Whenever the aim is to create floor plans that generate familiarity, the architects impress on account of their faculty for abiding by elementary spatial figures. "There are no complex and spectacular spatial creations in our projects," says Roger Diener. "We use simple, known typologies that have already proved their worth."[21] Complexity, in Diener & Diener's architecture, is never spatial. Yet a stance that apprehends any eye-catching treatment of space as modish rather than enriching need not rule it out. The complexity simply takes place at a different level, specifically in how the relationship between the rooms is expressed and what it signifies.

This expression is conveyed not just through space, but also through those traditional elements by which space is shaped. When Roger Diener repeats floor plans, he also repeats the use of standard elements such as doors, walls, windows, and fittings. To the extent that architects deliberately draw on a catalog—albeit a catalog of a high order—they reinforce the sense that they have mastered the ordinary. The dwelling, as we have said, is a place of conventions.

Yet we can still ask ourselves what Diener & Diener actually intend when they apply such standards. As we understand it, the expression of ordinariness is above all an attempt to show things for what they are. Liberating things from all those elements that are liable to alienate them allows them to be seen for what they are. A door is a door as long as it is perceived as such. Being inclined to objectivity, this stance approximates the architecture of the 1920s that came to be known as *Neue Sachlichkeit*.[22]

While many of today's architects look to the semiotic methods of the 1960s for cues,[23] Diener & Diener stand out precisely because of the absence of such signs in their architecture—or rather, to quote Steinmann, because of the "presence of empty signs."[24] These empty, objective signs have a special place in contemporary architecture as they resist the current tendency to invent a narrative for every project. "Buildings do not tell stories," says Roger Diener.[25] Hence they need not be perceived as such in respect of what they mean.

An architecture for the city

Ideas of the city and the theories that grow out of them develop in the course of time. Diener & Diener's first projects belong to the specific theoretical context defined by the 1966 publication of Aldo Rossi's *L'architettura della città*,[26] a work that championed an understanding of the city as living, historical

20 We are thinking here, among others, of Martin Steinmann, "Le sens du banal. Immeuble de bureaux de Diener & Diener à la Hochstrasse," in *Faces*, no. 13 (1989), pp. 6–11, about Diener & Diener's office building on Hochstrasse.
21 Diener September 1992, (see note 13).
22 Roger Diener has acknowledged the influence of Neues Bauen on his work on several occasions; see also Joseph Abram, "L'École de Bâle. Diener & Diener—de la Neue Sachlichkeit au réalisme contemporain," in *From City to Detail. Selected Buildings and Projects by Diener & Diener Architekten*, London/Berlin 1992, pp. 8–21; and Joseph Abram, "The Beauty of the Real," in *Diener & Diener*, London 2011, pp. 7–33.
23 We are thinking in particular of the writings of Roland Barthes, *Le degré zéro de l'écriture*, Paris 1953 (*Writing Degree Zero*, London 1967) and *Mythologies*, Paris 1957 (*Mythologies*, London 1972), and of Umberto Eco, *Trattato di semiotica generale*, Milan 1975 (*A Theory of Semiotics*, Bloomington, IN, 1976).
24 This is the expression that Martin Steinmann uses in his essay on the office building on Hochstrasse, (see note 20), pp. 6–11. We are of the opinion that this holds true for most projects by Diener & Diener, and for their housing projects especially.
25 Roger Diener, lecture to the Royal Institute of British Architects (RIBA), London, March 1992, typescript, archive Roger Diener.
26 Aldo Rossi, *L'architettura della città*, Padua 1966 (*Architecture of the City*, Cambridge, MA, 1982).

St. Alban-Tal, Basel, 1984–1986

material, and that shaped a whole generation of architects, as did Rossi's teaching at ETH Zurich.[27] Although Roger Diener was not a student of his, Rossi's ideas have certainly had an enduring influence on his understanding of the city through the concept of typology. He seeks to understand the various layers that together form the urban fabric of a place in order to be able to respond to these with a project that takes account of them in their totality. Instead of embarking on a wide-ranging study, however, he simply observes those traces that have accreted over the years as they manifest themselves today.

Twenty years after Rossi's book, Bernard Huet denounced what he saw as the essential disparity between architecture and city. His essay "L'architecture contre la ville" contains the following passage: "The city is a collective and plural fact; it is the expression of the public values of a community. Architecture is an individual and singular fact based on the particular and private vision of an individual or a group of individuals."[28] Architecture does not have the capacity to continue building the city, Huet argued, since it defends individual expression at the community's expense. This is not true of the architecture of Diener & Diener, however, which on the contrary seeks to reconcile the two. Huet ended his reflections on a positive note that we find confirmed in the work of Diener & Diener, conceding that "some architects, and not the least of them, are ready to accept a new situation in which the architect disappears in the face of the evidence of the architecture and the architecture in the face of the necessity of the city."[29]

The relationship to the city

These theoretical ideas may define the zeitgeist into which architecture is inscribed, but they do not say anything about the architect's share in it or his or her relationship to the city. According to Roger Diener, one key aspect of the architecture of Diener & Diener is the aspect of time. "It is all about apprehending a design not as the creative act of one particular instant—which may have grown out of an awareness of architectural history even if the underlying premise is still that of the project as autonomous and unique and hence also a form of artistic production—but rather as something developed out of an understanding of the design of buildings as embedded in the much larger process by which the city or urbanized landscape is transformed."[30]

The notion of the project as a statement made in a timeframe comprising successive layers of urban transformation is thus essential to any understanding of Diener & Diener's architecture. History is understood not as a sequence of significant events, but rather as the conditions prevailing at a certain moment that is itself the product of past events. This lends the project a firm basis inasmuch as it grounds reflection in permanence. It enters into a dialogue with previous events because it changes them and because it creates what, to all intents and purposes, is a new urban situation.

Taking account of the temporality of the place and understanding the development of a city by implanting something new into it does not have to lead to any obvious outcome. At issue is the balance struck between the different givens,

27 Aldo Rossi taught at ETH Zurich from 1972–1974 and from 1976–1978; see Ákos Moravánsky, Judith Hopfengärtner, *Aldo Rossi und die Schweiz—Architektonische Wechselwirkungen*, Zurich 2011. Roger Diener was not a student of his, but did attend his lectures; see the booklet on the film by Françoise Arnold, *L'Hypothèse Aldo Rossi*, Paris 2012, pp. 104–113.
28 Bernard Huet, "L'architecture contre la ville," in *AMC*, no. 14 (1986), pp. 10–14, quoted by Martin Steinmann, "Notate zur Architektur von Diener & Diener," in Roger Diener and Martin Steinmann, *Das Haus und die Stadt*, Lucerne 1995, p. 11, and used by Roger Diener in various lectures and talks.
29 Huet 1986, (see note 28).
30 Roger Diener, "*Über die Zeit gesehen*," lecture, Dortmund, October 2013, typescript, archive Roger Diener.

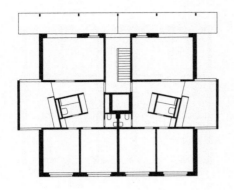

Riehenring, Basel, 1980–1985

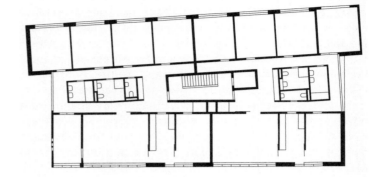

St. Alban-Tal, Basel, 1984–1986

which is what Roger Diener is striving for when he says: "Urban figure, building type, structure, and architectural elaboration are the means we place at our disposal. It is with them that we try to assemble an architecture—which by its very nature is discontinuous—in such a way that it can unfold its impact without threatening the equilibrium of the city and its historical substance."[31] This equilibrium, of course, is always uncertain, since it demands that a project be inscribed into, and hence connected to, historical layers, while at the same time being a project in its own right. Depending on the givens of the place, certain projects almost disappear, whereas others remain clearly apparent.

With his sure feel for synthesis, Vittorio Magnago Lampugnani identified the two types of urban development that, depending on the place, Diener & Diener use: the freestanding building and the building as "infill."[32] The categories are not clear cut as a rule, but rather tend to fluctuate. Thus we quite often notice leaps or ruptures in the infill that inevitably lend the building a kind of autonomy vis à vis those adjoining it. The freestanding building, by contrast, maintains a strong and complex spatial relationship with its surroundings. It is at this juncture that Steinmann reminds us that as a volume, such a building is bound to seek a dialectical relationship with the place: "Roger Diener has described this problem as follows: The aim is to bring order to the place with a single building. To this end, a more general relationship to the place must be sought by means of an autonomous building that incorporates what is there—albeit into its own logic, its own shape."[33]

The project as an inflection of typologies

The question still to be addressed once we have defined what we mean by typological design and "architecture for the city" is that of the synthesis that finds its confirmation in the architectural project. Diener & Diener's stance is determined not by theory, but by the individual project, which allows them to refine, confirm, or refute certain assumptions, even as it strikes its own balance between typology and city.

This is how we understand what Roger Diener said about his complex relationship both to the city and to architecture in a lecture he gave in Braunschweig in 2013: "And the reasons for all this? There are at least two that I would like to mention here: The first concerns the idea of a city that is subject to constant transformation, but that nevertheless has the capacity to uphold its identity. This also concerns the identity of specific urban spaces—and landscapes, too, to the extent that these are urbanized. We want our projects to consolidate this identity, by which I mean reinforce or even accentuate it. The second reason has to do with design itself. The confrontation that is essential to the program, here that of new housing with the structures already existing in a specific place, gives rise to new correlations and new constellations. This means that far from imposing restrictions on the new, our holding fast to the identity of what was there on the contrary proves to be an enrichment. Designs emerge that we could not, and would not, have been able to develop solely out of the theme of housing alone."[34]

Having acknowledged that the relationship between typology and place, if it is to develop, is one that requires constant realignment, which in turn engenders a sense of great continuity over time, the task now must be to map out those recurrent typologies in Diener & Diener's housing that might count as representative of their approach to design. These typologies, lined up alongside each other, also offer a revealing view of Diener & Diener's output to date. The intervals separating each use vary and illustrate very clearly how in the early days of the partnership, many questions were still in flux, necessitating corrections later on.

The premises of typological research

Roger Diener's arrival in his father's architect's office in 1976 signaled the beginning of intensive typological research that took on concrete form in his very first works.[35] While the tendency to repeat typologies is not yet apparent in these early projects, the interest in floor plans consisting of several spatial layers is evident.

---

31 Diener September 1992, (see note 13).
32 Lampugnani 1998, (see note 2), p.15ff.
33 Martin Steinmann in conversation with Jacques Lucan, in *Matière d'art—architecture contemporaine en Suisse*, catalog of the exhibition at Centre Culturel Suisse in Paris, Basel 2001, p.18.

34 Diener 2013, (see note 30).
35 Roger Diener's joining of his father's office in 1976 in our view marked a fresh start of its work in the housing sector; see Martin Steinmann's essay in this book, pp.31–43.

In Hammerstrasse (1978–1981), Roger Diener's first major housing project, buildings erected along three streets transformed an abandoned industrial site into a perimeter block development. As much as the apartments differ, they all feature the same division of the space between street and courtyard into three distinct layers: bedrooms/service areas/living areas. The neighboring development, Riehenring (1980–1985), differs in many respects, but features the same urban development form and the same internal organization of space. Here, however, the bedrooms face onto the quiet inner courtyard, while the living areas face onto the street and city. Each apartment ends in a balcony, which is positioned not according to the contrast between street and courtyard, but according to the sun.

The floor plan in three layers with the service areas in the middle is taken a stage further in the St. Alban-Tal development (1981–1986), specifically in the building that faces the Rhine promenade. Living room, kitchen, and dining room here form an enfilade, whose continuity is further reinforced by sliding doors. The service layer inside the apartment consists of a single, generously dimensioned hall occupied by the bathrooms. This hall also forms an elaborate access system, which as in Riehenring separates the bedrooms at the rear from the living areas.

Such an access system is wholly appropriate to apartments of this size, even if it makes for a less economical floor plan. The first optimization of it is evident in the second residential building, situated on the industrial canal. There, the bathrooms are situated next to the stairwell and there is only one point of entry to the remaining rooms. In all other respects, however, the functions follow an analogous order. The communal part of the apartment contains a kitchen, dining room, and living room, which here plays the role of a place. A built-in closet shields the bedrooms, but preserves this spatial continuity. This was a measure that Diener & Diener also applied to a residential building on Burgfelderplatz (1982–1985) dating from the same period, in which this space as the point of entry to the whole dwelling is affirmed even more strongly. There, too, the bedrooms are situated at the rear, facing onto a small courtyard, in order to distance them from the street.

The Warteck Plan

A first project on the former site of Basel's Warteck brewery envisaged a perimeter block development that was not pursued.[36] Diener & Diener's own 1991 project for the site is actually very close to the form of the development eventually realized (1992–1996). The floor plans of the apartment block differ significantly, however, as they are layered and have a bathroom core around which they are structured. The various radical measures adopted presumably served to bring the project into line with the standards applicable for subsidized housing. The most important of these entailed shifting the service areas to endow the floor plan with a central space—or "place," to borrow Josef Frank's term—with control of all the rooms. The decision to in-

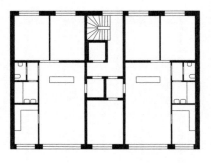

Warteckhof, Basel, 1992–1996

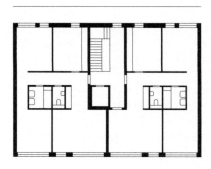

Warteckhof, Basel, 1991

corporate the access system into this space not only lends the apartments greater depth, but it also assures them of a domestic center.[37] The concentration of functions around a single space in a tightly controlled order lends the Warteck Plan great solidity, as if nothing might be either added or taken away from it.

The Warteckhof also concretizes an urban development form that according to Steinmann can be understood as a constellation.[38] And it is indeed the case that the apartment block interacts subtly both with the office building, which is likewise the work of Diener & Diener, and with the two old brewery buildings that are now protected historical monuments. While the building line on Grenzacherstrasse is rigorously upheld, the deviations from the same on the other sides—legible in the cobbling—blur our perception of the development as a straightforward perimeter block and emphasize the autonomy of each volume, while opening up the site to passersby.

Warteckhof B (1992), a project that was not built and has never been published, envisaged an apartment block with courtyard and hence can be viewed as a stage en route from the version of 1991 to the version of the Warteckhof actually

---

36 The first project, which was not by Diener & Diener, envisaged a perimeter block development on the whole of the Warteck Areal. Local opposition to the demolition of the old brewery buildings, however, led to a second project that preserved the most important of them without reducing the total floor area created.

37 On the subject of the home in Swiss housing, see Alexandre Aviolat, "Foyer—la conscience de la centralité," in *A l'intérieur*, Christophe Joud (ed.), *Cahier de théorie*, vol. 13, Lausanne 2016, pp. 60–77.
38 On the subject of the constellation, see Steinmann 1995, (see note 28).

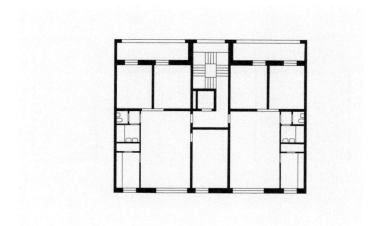

Warteckhof B, Basel, 1992

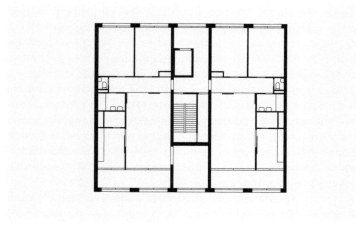

KNSM and Java-Island, Amsterdam, 1995–2001

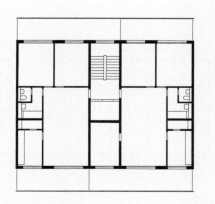

Hochbergerstrasse, Basel, 1993–2002

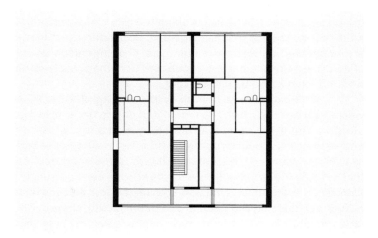

Ypenburg, The Hague, 2000–2003

built.[39] Here, the floor plans differ only slightly; the balconies look like relics of those of 1991, while the stairwells are a hybrid of the two versions. The Warteck Plan was also adopted for the Hochbergerstrasse development (1993–2002): a freestanding, eight-story apartment block that was designed shortly after the Warteckhof, but built only much later. The floor plan of the apartments is the same, except that they now have a storeroom behind the kitchen. The staircase has swapped places, while the entrance hall has disappeared altogether and the additional room now adjoins the central space. These minor modifications were necessitated by the form of the development, which in turn was defined by the boundaries of the site.

The solution selected appears to be the most rational since it reduces the dimensions wherever possible, specifically between the apartments. The disappearance of the entrance hall is a consequence of the staircase, which, having two flights, results in greater depth. Here, the "posh" entrance hall is omitted altogether, although tenants are of course at liberty to create such a space by means of a large closet. Most important of all, the relationship between inside and outside is a very different one here, where deep balconies along the façades on both sides of the building serve to filter out the city.

39 Warteckhof B is situated to the east of the Warteckhof on a site formerly belonging to the brewery.

The exported Warteck Plan

While the first three large projects with this floor plan belong to the special category of housing in Switzerland, Diener & Diener went on to experiment with the Warteck Plan in three major developments in Germany and Holland. Taking this floor plan as an example, we intend to show that a typology—that represents an abstraction—can also be concretized in places whose social and economic conditions are different.

Diener & Diener adopted the Warteck Plan for the elongated apartment block that they designed for Java-Island (1995–2001) in the port of Amsterdam, where it is positioned at a right angle to the bridge. Its form is linear, although the indentations in the façade lend it a more complex relationship to its location, thus recalling other, earlier projects by the architects, such as their study for Nielsen-Bohny in Basel in 1993. The stepped façade also informed the residential buildings planned for the Stückfärberei Areal in Basel in 1993, but not built, and, on a much larger scale, an urban study for the former gas works in Biel/Bienne conducted a year later.

In these projects, Diener & Diener proposed several residential buildings whose form interacts with the place, creating spaces of different width between the buildings. The indentations were not without typological consequences, however: The linear building in Amsterdam ranges between 8 and 25 m deep, and a special variant of the floor plan had to be developed for its narrowest point. In the 16-m-deep central parts, however, the Warteck Plan is inflected accordingly. A corridor separates the bedrooms from the living areas, which owing to the weather conditions prevailing in the port open onto verandas. Even if the corridor is very open, it still marks a break in depth that serves as an entrance hall and hence avoids a situation like that on Hochbergerstrasse. The greater depth at either end of the building results in floor plans that are adapted accordingly. The apartments facing north are minimized in depth to take account of the lack of sunlight, while the duplexes in the south retain the same depth, but with the service areas located at the rear.

Greater depth was a factor in Diener & Diener's work in Berlin, too, specifically its Parkkolonnaden development (1994–2000) consisting of two L-shaped blocks with an open courtyard at the head of Giorgio Grassi's master plan. Among the many different floor plans that were intermingled here is the Warteck Plan, whose hall is delimited by a closet, while the kitchen is wide open to the living room. The duplex apartments are positioned opposite the staircase. This ingenious layout allows three apartments to be accessed from the same landing, which is illuminated by natural light.

The residential high-rises in Ypenburg (2000–2003) were likewise faced with the problem of depth. Here, as in Amsterdam, the living room is enlarged by a veranda, while the entrance hall is articulated as a corridor, which keeps the bedrooms at a distance. This runs the depth of the apartment so that not only the bathroom, but also the kitchen can be arranged along it, far away from the façade. Presumably this accords with both Dutch building regulations and Dutch habits, since in Holland the kitchen is frequently regarded as a service area that can be banished deep inside the dwelling.[40] This kitchen, which is larger than a kitchenette, results in differently sized bedrooms: a large one for the parents and a smaller one for children. While such a hierarchy may be common in housing generally, it certainly is not in the works of Diener & Diener, whose floor plans generally feature rooms of equal size.

The Bener Plan

Diener & Diener proposed several different volumes for the competition for the development of the Bener Areal in Chur (1985), although their project is best known for the three small buildings that interpret the traditional Bündner typology. Here, however, our focus will be on the elongated residential building that follows the line of the railway tracks. The apartments inside this building have a corridor that affords access to the bedrooms on the one side and to the service areas on the other, and that at the end opens out into a combined living and dining area. The advantage of this rational, Modernist-inspired layout is that it responds to the specific conditions of the site. The rooms serving functions that count as less sensitive face onto the noisy tracks, whereas all the other rooms face onto the garden. This clear contrast between the two sides also applies to sunlight. Large loggias, essentially outdoor rooms, enhance the view that in the living room extends from the garden all the way

Bener-Area, Chur, 1985

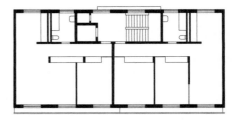

Schönaustrasse, Basel, 1996–2002

to the tracks. Another Modernist element are the posts that divide up the communal space—a layout that recalls Mies van der Rohe's House with Three Patios (1934).[41]

Even more than its Modernist pedigree, it is this floor plan's capacity to adapt to the limitations of a given site that makes it a typology that Diener & Diener, responding to the specifics of a given site, have repeated in several different projects and with greater variations than the Warteck Plan. On Schönaustrasse (1996–2002) in Basel, for example, the row that completes the perimeter block consists of Bener-type apartments. There, too, the service areas, including the staircase, face onto the street, whereas all the other rooms face onto the courtyard at the rear. The floor plan is more radical than that for the Bener Areal, however, because the rooms face north. The justification for this layout was the need to comply with noise protection regulations; at least the large kitchen brings sunlight into the living room.

Whereas only with difficulty can the Warteck Plan admit access to more than two apartments per story, the elongated Bener Plan offers the possibility of adding a third apartment facing in one direction only. One early example of this is the building on Elsässerstrasse (1996–1997) in Basel, which is situated at the corner of a perimeter block development and

---

40 Both the courtyard development by Hans Kollhoff (1994) adjoining it and The Whale by De Architecten Cie. (2000) on the other side of the dam—to name just two examples—situate the kitchen in the middle of the apartment and hence in the dark.

41 There is an explicit reference to this project by Mies van der Rohe in the competition plans.

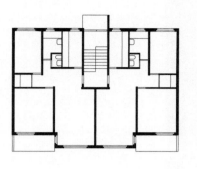

Ernst Göhner, Plan G2, 1965

Hardhof, Bülach, 2013–2019

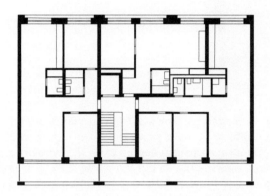

GreenCity, Zurich, 2012–2018

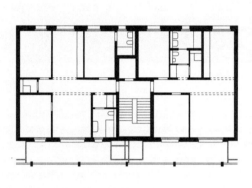

Weidmatt B3, Lausen and Liestal, 2014–2020

demonstrates how the choice of typology is also dependent on the site. Since its situation prevents windows facing onto the courtyard, the service areas here form a layer along the firewall and courtyard wall, while the living room and bedrooms face onto the street. This makes it a special, site-specific variant of the Bener Plan, which anticipates the more economical arrangement of three units per story that would characterize subsequent projects.

The Göhner Plan

Looking at Diener & Diener's more recent projects, we notice how the two typologies discussed are gradually being abandoned in favor of a floor plan that is familiar to us and that we shall call the Göhner Plan. Why this reference to Ernst Göhner, a figure that no discussion of the rationalization of housing can afford to ignore? According to Roger Diener, the floor plan that Diener & Diener used in these projects was tinged by nostalgia. The Göhner Plan, the G2 plan developed in 1965 for the IGECO system of prefabrication, basically matched what had long been the standard floor plan consisting of a corridor with rooms on either side of it. Only now the living room opened onto the entrance hall, and the kitchen had a glass door to allow light from the other side to enter the living room. (As with the Warteck Plan, there is no separate entrance hall as such.) The day rooms are thus kept clearly separate from the night rooms.

The first inflection of this plan is to be found in a residential building in GreenCity, Zurich-Manegg (2018), incidentally alongside examples of both the Warteck and the Bener Plan, making it a typological show cabinet. The large, U-shaped building forms part of a development plan by Diener & Diener, which with still more such volumes is spreading along the foot of the Entlisberg. Responding to the topographical givens, they all have courtyards that open onto the wooded hillside. The nucleus of the new district is a plaza where a repurposed factory—the nineteenth-century spinning mill that was the largest of its kind in Canton Zurich at the time—recalls its industrial past. These apartments diverge from the Göhnerswil floor plan in at least one major respect. They are accessed in the area of the bedrooms, which runs counter to what was customary in the 1960s. At the other end of the apartment is a space that faces in both directions and that is divided by the projecting bathrooms into an eat-in kitchen and a living room. The long, uninterrupted wall enhances the apartment's permeability.

Our next examples of the Göhner Plan are the three Hardhof residential buildings on the site of the former Sulzer foundry in Bülach (2013–2019). Here, too, the development plan was the work of Diener & Diener, which subsequently designed the residential buildings for one of the plots. The floor plans of these buildings, which together form a courtyard, constitute a further development of the Göhner Plan, thus demonstrating its capacity to adapt to particular situations.

Favrehof, Wallisellen, 2008–2014

The project studies of 2013 help us to understand this development as they show how the initial floor plan of the longest of the three buildings was compressed during the design process, undoubtedly to reduce floor area and hence costs. But how might the typology be adapted in line with such economic constraints? The most important adaptation consisted in the substitution of the eat-in kitchen with a purely functional kitchen. This in turn changes the look of the living area, which, as in the Warteck Plan, now forms the center of the apartment—an effect that is further enhanced by wide French windows opening onto the deep balcony. The permeability of the apartment that is a characteristic feature of the Göhner Plan is again confirmed by the long wall.

The two other residential buildings that form the corner of the site on Schaffhauserstrasse are connected by a wall to shield the courtyard from noise. Their floor plans are quite obviously a realization of the Göhner Plan, even if there is no door separating the kitchen from the living room. There is one significant change, however: the apartments are all accessed along the façade, which in the work of Diener & Diener is an unusual solution and was selected here on account of the noise. The entrance hall leads not only into the living room—whose role as place is thereby enhanced—but also onto a veranda, which here does not constitute an extension of the living room.

One last example of the many different ways in which the Göhner Plan has been inflected that warrants mention is Weidmatt in Lausen and Liestal. This development, which comprises ten buildings with over a hundred units (2014–2020), is being built on the site of a former explosives factory.[42] According to an earlier, subsequently abandoned study, Diener & Diener initially envisaged two rows of three- to six-story buildings of varying depth to be built along the River Ergolz. While at first we may be struck by what seems to be the typological diversity of these apartments, in our view they can be classified according to just a few salient features and hence demonstrate how the architects understand, and work with, the concept of typology. Buildings C4 and B3 are the ones with the greatest affinity to the Göhner Plan. Here, we again find the through space made up of a living room and a rather narrow eat-in kitchen. This communal space also affords access to the two bedrooms, the foremost of which is accessed via a sliding door, which besides allowing it to be used in a wide range of ways also generates a sense of space.

Looking at a third-floor plan, that of the C3 buildings, we again find a through space, the front part of which narrows into a dining area. The bathrooms, meanwhile, are arranged so that they form a core, which, as in St. Alban-Tal, has to be walked around, except that here this is done through the kitchen, which is situated on the façade. As a typology, this floor plan is certainly not unknown in contemporary housing in Switzerland. We have only to think of Gigon Guyer's development on the site of the former nursing school in Zurich (1998–2002) to find an example. In Weidmatt, however, it is combined with features drawn from the Göhner Plan, thanks to which one crucial factor is thrown into relief: as a typology always arises out of certain cultural needs, when those needs change, there has to be a change of floor plan—a change that may be so far-reaching that it is tantamount to a completely new typology. This seems to be the case here, even if the Göhner Plan continues to shine through, rather like a palimpsest.

We encounter the inflection of another type in the C1 building, which we shall discuss presently. Weidmatt thus turns out to be a kind of experimental development along the lines of the Weissenhofsiedlung in Stuttgart of 1927 or Karlsruhe-Dammerstock, the purpose in each case having been to

---

42 After the production of explosives was discontinued in 1999, the municipalities of Lausen and Liestal decided to use the site to build new housing. Several investors had a share in the project, the overall planning of which was done by Diener & Diener.

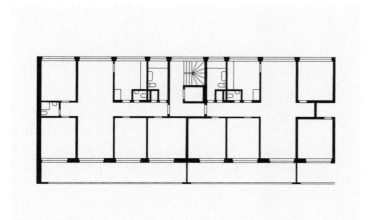

Nielsen-Bohny, Basel, 1993.

Schönwil, Meggen, 2006–2012

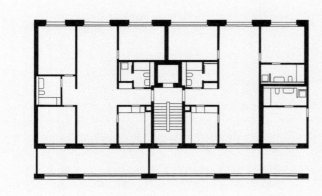

Favrehof, Wallisellen, 2008–2014

Weidmatt C1, Lausen and Liestal, 2014–2020

investigate human habitats in the *âge du machinisme* on the basis of built case studies. Diener & Diener's residential buildings do not make such claims for themselves, of course; but in an age in which habits are diversifying, ostensibly rendering typological design meaningless, their inventive inflection of just a few typologies proves just how unfounded this opinion is.

The Nielsen-Bohny Plan

The last type we shall discuss here came to our attention while we were studying the Favrehof (2008–2014) in Wallisellen. This floor plan is remarkable for its living rooms spanning the entire apartment. Roger Diener calls them "drive-through living rooms."[43] Surprisingly, this typology occurs only once in Diener & Diener's housing projects, even though it has been customary in Swiss housing for some time now. Searching through their archives, however, we do in fact find a comparable floor plan in a 1993 study undertaken for the company Nielsen-Bohny that was mentioned above in connection with the shape of the Amsterdam project. It would appear that twenty years on, the architects are at last returning to this type.

Diener & Diener's project occupies a plot to the south of Wallisellen railway station on a site whose development plan was the work of Lampugnani. Inspired by the idea of the

43 Roger Diener, explanation of the project, archive Diener & Diener.

nineteenth-century European city, it consists of variously shaped residential buildings erected around courtyards, which together form a unique urban district in the middle of suburbia. The apartments of the Favrehof are all identical and all feature the through living room mentioned above. The balconies on three sides face onto the central courtyard, while the fourth side faces onto the street running through the district. Here, too, the living room affords access to the bedrooms, while the kitchen is situated to one side of it and initially had doors shutting it off from both living room and entrance hall. As built, however, it is more like a niche.

But we can also see this floor plan as an inflection of a different type, first used in two small residential buildings Schönwil in Meggen (2006–2012). These—one with three, the other with two apartments per story—stand side by side and slightly offset in the park of a nineteenth-century villa. The apartments they contain each have two or three rooms facing out back. The outer room is connected to the living room by double doors, allowing it to be used as an extension of the same as and when needed. So a through space can be created here, too. The floor plan of the apartments differs from the Göhner Plan inasmuch as the kitchen is situated alongside the living room and has sliding doors that lend the latter an elevated status.

A similar floor plan is to be found in the C1 building of the Weidmatt development in Lausen and Liestal discussed above. Here, too, the room accessed from the living room has double doors. The difference between this floor plan and the apartments in Meggen, however, is the kitchen that is wide open to the living room. This allows the living area to be viewed in two ways: on the one hand along the axis of depth and on the other across its breadth where two French windows lead out onto the balcony.

A conclusion of sorts

What does this teach us about the working method that Diener & Diener bring to bear on their projects? First, it teaches us that for the past forty years, their thinking about housing has rested on the inflection of just a few typologies. Those typologies, whose development can be followed throughout the twentieth century, have proven their worth in practice owing to their capacity to respond to the manifold economic and social factors that determine contemporary housing and to different urban forms. Diener & Diener's radical position thus calls into question those notions that in more recent housing projects have driven architects to "invent" new floor plans for every project, which inevitably means jettisoning universal solutions.

What Diener & Diener also teach us, moreover, is that it is not enough merely to inflect a typology as such, since its relationship with its place must be redefined on a case-by-case basis. This relationship enriches the typology by making it part of the ever-changing continuum of the city. A new building is an addition that can be read at once as something new and as something which, being contingent on the location, continues what was there before. The constant quest, therefore, must be for an "unstable equilibrium" between what is there and what is to be added. This is how cities develop and this is also how Diener & Diener's architecture evolves.

As we are talking here about housing, that architecture also impacts decisions affecting society as a whole. Viewed in this light, the use of typologies is not without ramifications, as it demands an ever-new understanding of habits and how these might be formalized in architecture. As habits often resist the straitjacket into which we try to squeeze them and seem to change only very slowly, typologies still offer a reliable way of responding to problems that are essentially societal in nature. That is why Diener & Diener's work seems to us to be of great importance to any reflections on housing in our time, even if such reflections themselves are becoming increasingly questionable, as Roger Diener himself has noted: "It is at any rate becoming harder for us as architects to identify any socially and culturally relevant contribution in our work."[44]

---

44 Roger Diener, "Konvention: Einsiedler Architekturtage," lecture, October 2008, archive Roger Diener.

Marcus Diener Architekt
Housing in Basel after World War II

Martin Steinmann

*"Pour qu'une chose soit intéressante,
il suffit de la regarder longtemps."*
Gustave Flaubert

Ever since the completion of the first residential development for which Roger Diener alone was responsible on Hammerstrasse in Basel in 1978–1981, the designs of the office that from 1980 onward would call itself Diener & Diener have been making what in many respects is a fundamental contribution to urban housing. The one constant that sets them apart from many other housing projects realized in Switzerland during the same period is their reflection on elementary forms of dwelling. These forms should be understood as types, that is, as a means of both classifying use according to its essentials and of assuring the dwelling of a structure predicated on use.[1]

This typological approach to housing belongs to a tradition that for centuries was a matter of course and that not even Neues Bauen with its studies of the dwelling called into question. The key difference lies in the replacement of the pragmatism that had held sway prior to the First World War with a reliance on scientific methods and specifically the "motion studies" of Frederick Taylor, as manifested in the studies of Alexander Klein and the floor plans he derived from them, to name just one example. In his influential book of 1911, *The Principles of Scientific Management*, Taylor wasted no time in proposing that his principles be applied to private households, too.[2]

A quick glance at history is enough to show how the "normal dwelling" has in fact been formed—and deformed—by various conditions. Both needs themselves and the means by which they are satisfied coalesce to form types, i.e. spatial and material structures that reference what Le Corbusier called the *"solutions-types"* of a given period. This is what defines the general character of a dwelling that has to satisfy the needs of the masses. Starting in the 1920s, the development of housing for a long time followed an objective tradition and studiously avoided "inventions" of the kind that proliferate today.

As Roger Diener has pointed out: "When we compare the floor plans of the developments built before World War II with those that came after it, we notice an astonishing consistency. Not even the more recent examples that have brought methodical housing back into the city differ significantly from those earlier examples [...] The needs a dwelling has to satisfy seem not to have changed for a long time."[3] He then adds, by way of an afterthought, that this seems to be changing now.

The beginnings

There was a personal element to Roger Diener's comment on the very slow development of housing: specifically the work of his father in this field, which is the reason for this essay in what is actually a book about Diener & Diener's housing projects. Marcus Diener built several thousand dwellings both in Basel itself and in neighboring municipalities in the decades following the founding of his architect's office in Basel in 1942. These allow us to accurately reconstruct how housing in Switzerland developed after World War II, taking account of not just the architectural aspects, but also the technical, economic, and social changes that defined those decades.

In a private publication about his father's work, Roger Diener remarks on how well it lends itself to a description of these developments since "it touches on all the important programs of the period: the building of residential buildings on a large scale"— i.e. on the periphery—"and the remodeling of residential buildings in the city itself. These are the buildings that leave their stamp on the city and its districts. That is what makes them important, and a reflection of the conditions prevailing at the time they were built."[4] The residential buildings of three successive decades that have influenced not just the look of the city in certain places, but also a range of sociological factors will be discussed in what follows.

Marcus Diener was born in Basel on September 24, 1918, and went to school there, too. Since he had to learn a trade, he left high school before graduating and embarked on a three-year apprenticeship as an architectural draftsman at Alban Werdenberg in Basel. He also attended courses taught by Hans Bernoulli, Georg Schmidt, and Hermann Baur at Basel School of Arts and Crafts. His apprenticeship ended in 1937 in the middle of an economic crisis when very little was being built. Unable to find work, he began hatching plans to emigrate to Australia, but was prevented from doing so by the outbreak of war in September 1939. Over the next few years he himself saw one thousand days of service as a private in an artillery regiment. It was while on leave for a few months in 1942 that he founded his own office together with Joseph Oberle, who being much older than him was probably exempt from military service and in any case pulled out of the partnership in 1950.[5] Since then, the name on the plans reads "Marcus Diener Architekt."

Subsidized housing

After some relatively small projects, Diener & Oberle won a contract from the Musikverein, which wanted to have a design by other architects for a large residential building at Schützenmattstrasse 33–35 in Basel reworked. This was Diener & Ober-

---

1 This aspect of the architecture of Diener & Diener is discussed by Alexandre Aviolat here in this book, pp. 19–30.
2 Frederick Taylor, *The Principles of Scientific Management*, New York/London 1911.
3 Roger Diener, "Urban Housing," lecture in Barcelona, 1996, typescript, archive Roger Diener.
4 Roger Diener, *Marcus Diener Architekt*, Basel 1978, p. 3.
5 Information kindly provided by Roger Diener.

le's first major contract and they completed it to their client's satisfaction. Otherwise, however, their list of works for those early years consists mainly of remodeling projects aimed at creating more living space. Responding to the housing shortage—construction having stagnated owing to the wartime rationing of building materials and the large number of builders mobilized for military service—the Swiss Federal Council in 1942 decided to subsidize the construction costs of new housing to the tune of 5 percent wherever the canton agreed to cover an additional 10 percent. Later that same year, the subsidy was raised to 10 percent of the construction costs for housing built by cooperatives.[6] Canton Basel-Stadt subsidized housing from 1943 onward.

No fewer than seventy-three new housing cooperatives were founded in the canton between 1943 and 1950 alone. Besides subsidizing the construction costs, the municipalities also leased land for the cooperatives to build on; and so the number of dwellings in their hands rose from 2,273 to 6,852 during the same period.[7] Yet the housing shortage lingered on, in part because the postwar marriage boom had led to an increase in births and in part because of the large influx of immigrants from other municipalities following the repeal of the 1941 curtailment of freedom of establishment. The housing cooperatives attracted a disproportionately large number of workers, civil servants, and salaried employees from both the public and the private sector. Yet the rents were relatively high—at least as long as the rent caps introduced during the war remained in force.

Although he never belonged to a party, Diener's political sympathies lay with the left and this naturally brought him into contact with the housing cooperatives. In fact, after 1946, Diener & Oberle's work for them would be their principal source of contracts for several years to come. Both were therefore present at the 1947 founding of the Holeestrasse housing cooperative, for which in 1949–1951 they would build three rows of four or five apartment blocks each.[8] Their first project for a cooperative, however, was in 1946, when they built a row of six, five-story blocks for the cooperative Zum Bischofstein, Basel, on the street of that name. The staircase in each block afforded access to two 3-room apartments per story, each of which had a familiar floor plan in which, to avoid wasting space on a corridor, one of the two bedrooms is accessed from the living room. This floor plan can be found in various residential developments both before and after World War II, among them the apartment blocks by Kellermüller & Hofmann on Zurlindenstrasse in Zurich of 1932.[9] It constitutes the most compact, and hence most economical, layout for an apartment of this size. Diener & Oberle built another row of buildings for the same cooperative on Oltingerstrasse in Basel later in 1946.

6 See Tim Cuénod, *Das kurze 'goldene' Jahrzehnt der Basler und die politischen Auseinandersetzungen um die Wohnraumspolitik 1943–1950*, degree thesis, Basel 2012, pp. 24. "Canton Basel-Stadt received Federal Government grants in the order of 20.9 million Swiss francs for its housing subsidies. And the grants paid by Canton Basel-Stadt itself totaled some 49.7 million Swiss francs, meaning that some 70.6 million Swiss francs were made available for building new housing. Using this sum, a total of 8,374 new apartments were built," Othmar Jauch, "Sozialer Wohnungsbau und staatliche Wohnbauförderung in Basel," in *Das Werk*, vol. 46, no. 1 (1959), p. 7.
7 Cuénod 2012, (see note 6), p. 30.
8 Minutes of the constitutive meeting of the Holee housing cooperative on June 20, 1947.
9 See Christoph Luchsinger, *Hans Hofmann—Vom Neuen Bauen zur neuen Baukunst*, Zurich 1985, pp. 60–61.

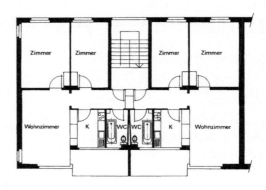

Kellermüller & Hofmann, residential buildings, Zurlindenstrasse Zurich, 1932

The development of the floor plan

With this first contract the office had proved itself to be reliable. The number of apartment blocks it was henceforth asked to build for still more cooperatives in both Basel and Riehen is remarkable. Their floor plans follow a familiar typology for working- and lower-middle-class homes. The rooms of the three- and four-room apartments are lined up along a corridor, which on the plans is called a *Vorplatz*, or vestibule. This was a typology that had evolved in the mid-nineteenth century. Often the rooms have connecting doors to broaden the scope of their potential uses. The toilets in these buildings, and later the bathrooms, are situated on the façade next to the kitchen as a rule. We shall return to the architecture of these developments.

The housing developed by Diener & Oberle and, after Oberle's departure in 1950, by Marcus Diener alone, features certain constants which are attributable to the buildings' greater depth, or which rather necessitated that greater depth. The first of these is the bathroom and its place in the floor plan. In developments with a building depth of about 10 m, it could have a window for both daylight and ventilation, as required by the building regulations of the time.[10] Mechanical ventilation was also possible, but costly. This all changed in response to the economic pressures of the 1950s. The residential buildings that Diener designed for Buchenstrasse in 1953, for example, were about 12 m deep. The bathrooms therefore had to be on the inside at the end of the corridor and artificially ventilated. This would henceforth be their standard position.

The next step entailed moving the staircase, too, deeper into the building. The statutory building depth of 16 m presented no obstacle here.[11] Two different floor plans were developed for the five apartment blocks designed by the office for a cooperative on Bäumlihofstrasse in Riehen: one had a bathroom with a window, the other an inside bathroom at the end of the corridor, but both had an inside staircase. On this point the building regulations were vague, demanding only that corridors and staircases "have a supply of light and air commensurate

10 Art. 137 *Hochbautengesetz des Kantons Basel-Stadt* of 1949: "In bathrooms the windows must open onto the outside or ample fresh air be provided in some other way."
11 Art. 12 Appendix: "This depth shall be: – in Zones 6 and 5: 18.00 m back from the building line; – in Zones 5a, 4, and 3: 16.00 m back from the building line."

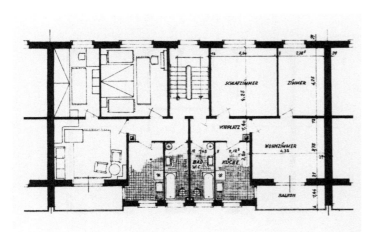

Diener & Oberle, residential buildings, Oltingerstrasse, Basel, 1946

Diener & Oberle, residential buildings, Oltingerstrasse, Basel, 1946

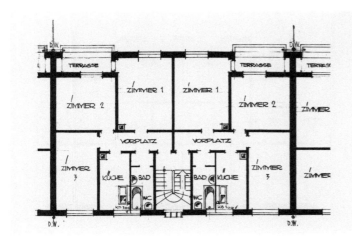

Diener & Oberle, residential buildings, Lörracherstrasse, Riehen, 1946–1947

Diener & Oberle, residential buildings, Lörracherstrasse, Riehen, 1946–1947

Diener & Oberle, residential buildings, Wittlingerstrasse, Basel, 1948

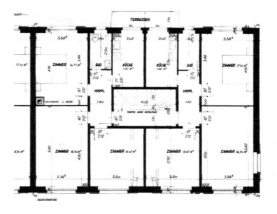

Marcus Diener, residential buildings, Bäumlihofstrasse, Riehen, 1953

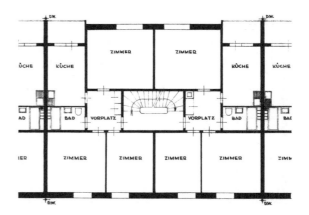

Marcus Diener, residential buildings, Bäumlihofstrasse, Riehen, 1957

Marcus Diener, residential buildings, Bäumlihofstrasse, Riehen, 1957

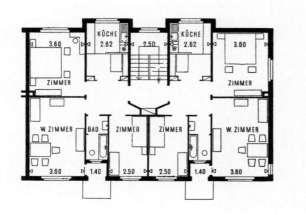

Müller & Egender, Sonnengarten development, Zurich, 1946

with their function."[12] In the aforementioned buildings, however, both spaces were in the dark. The purpose of such rearrangements, of course, was to reserve the windows for those rooms in which the inhabitants would spend most of their time. In other words, it was about making economical use of the land.

The floor plans vary the relationship between those few rooms whose use is not specified on the plans but which together comprise a "normal" family dwelling and the kitchen, bathroom, and balcony, which in the plans is called a *Terrasse*. These elements are related to each other via the corridor. Varying a floor plan essentially means changing the location of the said spaces relative to each other, or what might be called the "topography" of the dwelling. Such variations may be motivated by technical or practical considerations. Sometimes the kitchen and bathroom have to be adjoining as they share the same pipe shaft; sometimes they are kept separate with the kitchen next to a room with a balcony or opening onto the balcony itself, which would probably change its use and hence its importance to the dwelling as a whole. The balconies for the most part look out onto the garden, providing the residential blocks with their own "backyard" (as is borne out by the things typically kept there). But they are often too narrow to warrant the description "outdoor space." It follows that most of the alterations visible nowadays on the outside of these apartment blocks concern the balconies, whose depth has had to be increased in line with contemporary requirements.

Normal floor plans

"Normal," in this case, means two 3- or 4-room apartments per story, although there are also examples of more than two apartments per story, each with one or two rooms. Obviously, such small apartments are not intended for families.

In Marcus Diener's work they play a special role as dwellings for singles, who after all account for a large proportion of the urban population. We shall return to these shortly, but let us for the moment remain with those of Diener's apartment blocks that feature what Julius Maurizio called "normal floor plans."[13]

12 Art. 167. Diener & Oberle built three residential buildings with inside staircases at Ziegelhöfen 82–86 as early as 1946, although these were only 10.70 m deep.
13 Julius Maurizio, *Der Siedlungsbau in der Schweiz 1940–1950*, Erlenbach-Zurich 1952.

Attempts to open up the apartments on the inside by adding a dining area to the kitchen, which is what Karl Egender and Werner Müller did in the Sonnengarten apartments in Zurich of 1944–1946, are conspicuous by their absence.[14] But such experiments are never dependent on the architect alone, and very few housing cooperatives were receptive to floor plans that they believed would not be compatible with their members' habits.

Gustav Hassenpflug lamented this shortage of new dwelling forms in an article called "Neue Wege im Mietshausbau," published in *Bauen + Wohnen* in 1955. Unlike in the 1920s, housing associations were shying away from any innovations at all, he complained: "After the last war, the architects again expected the housing associations to do the pioneering work. They did not deliver. Indeed, some housing associations to this day refuse to build even established types, such as access-gallery blocks, and instead confine themselves to those few types that have ostensibly proved their worth over the decades."[15] Diener was to build two major developments with access-gallery blocks in the 1960s.

Yet the need for new floor plans to loosen up the apartments was no longer in dispute. How these might be obtained—by varying familiar floor plans, for example—was demonstrated by the aforementioned Sonnengarten development in Zurich and described in an essay by Otto H. Senn, published in *Das Werk* in 1962. The focus there was on the kitchen and its role in the apartment as a whole. The kitchen for work only—like the Frankfurt Kitchen—had a "bourgeois lineage," Senn argued. He compared it to attempts to combine cooking and eating in a single room, specifically "the good old *Wohnküche* [eat-in kitchen] and the *Kochkapelle* in the living room." The second of these, resembling a fume cupboard, was the more promising of the two, said Senn, hailing it as "a fluid sequence of spaces that can be partitioned off or flow into each other, in which cooking and eating are integrated into daily life."[16]

There was no such loosening up of floor plans in Diener's residential buildings, however. One notable exception are those in which the kitchen is accessed from the living room, which consequently counts as a *Wohnküche*. The kitchen itself is nevertheless small, hence the fume cupboard metaphor. Otherwise, Diener contents himself with updating the conventional floor plan by arranging the various spaces around the corridor or *Vorplatz*, but without connecting them directly. Just how much this typology—for all its apparent simplicity—might be varied is evident from a residential building that he erected at his own expense at Benkenstrasse 60 in Basel in 1949, one of whose first-floor apartments he took for himself and his family. The corridor here is wider than usual and is split into a hall giving onto the reception rooms and a part leading to all the others. It is his finest work in urban housing. Yet it must also be said that the apartments are designed for a rather bourgeois way of life, as is apparent from the large sliding doors separating the reception rooms.

14 "K. Egender and W. Müller, Stadtrandsiedlung Im Triemli, Zürich," in Maurizio 1962, (see note 13), pp.132–135.
15 Gustav Hassenpflug, "Neue Wege im Wohnungsbau," in *Bauen + Wohnen*, vol.9, no.3 (1955), p.216. Writing in the same vein in 1946, Alfred Roth remarked that instead of taking the floor plan as the principal object of study, architects were contenting themselves with conventional solutions in which the rooms were lined up along a narrow and gloomy corridor. Alfred Roth, "Bemerkungen zu drei neuen Siedlungen in Zürich," in *Das Werk*, vol.33, no.1 (1946), p.3.
16 Otto H. Senn, "Der Wohnungsgrundriss," in *Das Werk*, vol.50, no.1 (1963), pp.5–8.

Marcus Diener, residential building, Benkenstrasse, Basel, 1949

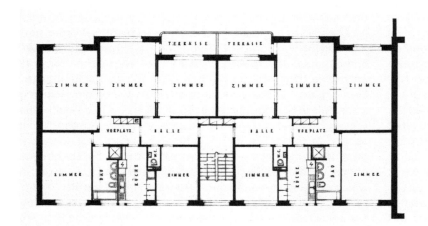
Marcus Diener, residential building, Benkenstrasse, Basel, 1949

Marcus Diener, residential building, Buchenstrasse, Basel, 1954

Marcus Diener, residential buildings, Buchenstrasse/Gotthelfstrasse, Basel, 1954

Homes for singles

The apartments that Marcus Diener built in the 1940s and 1950s generally had three or four rooms and were intended, as already mentioned, for families. There was nevertheless a demand for small apartments, too, which explains why Julius Maurizio, Basel's Cantonal Inspector of Buildings, felt bound to remark that the type and size of dwelling needed was a variable that changed constantly throughout people's lives. "These small apartments," he wrote, referring to those with two or three rooms, "are not only more crisis-resistant than large apartments, but they form a most necessary supplement to the same inasmuch as they provide a home for young couples, the numerous small families, and those elderly couples whose children have already left home."[17]

It is interesting that Maurizio made no mention of single men and women. Singles may have accounted for a large proportion of the populace at the time, but the developments presented in his book would scarcely have been the right milieu for them.[18] Nor did he discuss any one- and two-room apartments like those in the "Haus für alleinstehende Frauen" ("House for Single Women") built by Paul Artaria and Hans Schmidt in Basel in 1929.[19] With its communal facilities, that block actually came very close to the serviced apartments being built in American cities at the time. But even without the services, this type—which following the designation *Appartementhaus* used on some of the plans I shall refer to here as an "apartment house"—in fact constitutes a form of housing which was to play an important role in Diener's work of the 1950s.

Roger Diener believes his father became acquainted with this type of urban living during his first stay in the United States in 1950. As the history of such apartment houses in Switzerland has scarcely been researched at all, it is hard to say to what extent Diener's examples constituted a new typology. His list of works after 1951 certainly includes a remarkably large number of residential buildings with one- and two-room apartments arranged on both sides of a long, inside corridor, which right from the start was accessed by elevator. Unlike the buildings that Diener designed for the housing cooperatives, his apartment houses were all located in the city, not on the outskirts of Basel. The clients were different, too, being primarily consortia in which Diener himself often had a stake, along with others in the building trade, such as painters, builders, and even wreckers, given that many of the apartment houses were in fact replacing older buildings.

Strictly speaking, the first example of this new urban typology was the residential building on Schützenmattstrasse of 1943, which contained three two-room apartments with windows on one side only. Here, the rooms are arranged on either side of the kitchen and bathroom to form typological units, which at either end of the building are enlarged by the addition of a third room. This building already had an elevator, yet it cannot really be called an apartment house in the strict sense of the term that I am using here. That, it seems to me, does not really become applicable until 1951, when Diener built two residential buildings at Johannitergstrasse 13–15 in Basel. Yet there, too, the concept was still not that of serviced housing; it was rather a block of small units of just one room—in later buildings sometimes two rooms—each. Since the kitchens in these first apartment houses by Diener had a waste chute, however, it seems that at least some form of service had been provided after all.

The apartment houses

One of these buildings has has eight, the other four, single-room apartments per story, with elevator access. Adjoining the room is a service layer, the vestibule, bathroom, and kitchen. The kitchen projects outward forming one side of the balcony that extends across the full breadth of the room. The floor plan is very simple and clear, as are those for the variations of the one- and two-room typology applied in subsequent apartment houses. The bathroom is situated on the inside as a rule and in some cases is separate from the kitchen. One exception is the apartment house at Güterstrasse 83, where the kitchen is also situated on the inside, back-to-back with the bathroom. Since here it forms a niche that opens onto the room, it once again counts as a *Wohnküche* or eat-in kitchen; and because it is set back from the façade, the balcony can also be accessed from the bedroom, which projects somewhat and is just as wide as the living room.

Whether there were models for the typology of the apartment houses remains a moot point. Almost nothing was written about them in the 1950s, not even in architectural magazines such as *Das Werk* or *Bauen + Wohnen*. These were dwellings for a social class that wanted to live in the city where services were available nearby, even if not in the building itself.[20] I actually know of only one block of serviced apartments in the true sense of the word in 1950s Basel. Comprising furnished one-room apartments with services and communal spaces, it was built on Brunngässlein by the architects Bräuning, Leu, Dürig. And of all people it was Marcus Diener who in 1967 converted the business premises at the rear of the building into additional serviced apartments![21]

It was not the first one however. In 1934–1935 the architects Eckenstein and Kelterborn had built an apartment house called the Dufourhaus after the street on which it stood. When it was torn down in 1988, Roger Diener wrote an "obituary" to this iron-post construction: "The architects see in this program a contemporary answer to societal developments. The thirty or so rooms divided into various types were to answer the specific requirements of the individual tenants. The dumb-waiter (from the ground-floor restaurant, MS) served the various floors. To underscore the novelty of the type of dwelling the rooms were furnished with items from Wohnbedarf. There was also a top-floor common room and a terrace."[22]

---

17 Maurizio 1952, (see note 13), p. 34.
18 An essay concerned primarily with the situation of women contains the following passage: "The number of single women who are looking in vain for a suitable place to live is very large. Either they have to suffer the unpleasant aspects of a furnished or unfurnished room in someone else's apartment [...] or they have to wait until one of the few affordable small apartments the housing market has to offer becomes free, or have their name added to the list for an apartment house, should the rent be affordable at all." Berta Rahm, "Wohnmöglichkeiten für Alleinstehende," in *Das Werk*, vol. 57, no. 11 (1950), pp. 325–334, p. 327. The same applied to single men, too.
19 See Ursula Suter, *Hans Schmidt 1893–1972. Architekt in Basel, Moskau, Berlin-Ost*, Zurich 1993, pp. 182–185.
20 In the *Hochbautengesetz des Kantons Basel-Stadt* of 1949, these are described as follows: "Apartment houses are blocks of rented apartments with a communal dining room and kitchen and housekeeping services."
21 The apartment house at Brunngasse was transformed in 2014 by the architects Bucher, Bründler into the Hotel Nomad.
22 According to Roger Diener, "Die Montage der Ration Wohnung—zum

Marcus Diener, apartment houses, Johanniterstrasse, Basel, 1951

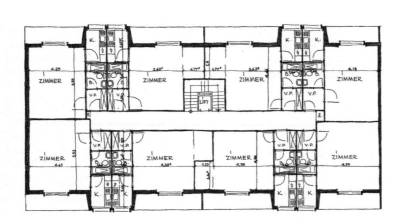

Marcus Diener, apartment houses, Johanniterstrasse, Basel, 1951

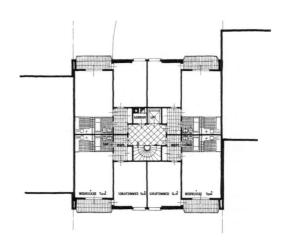

Marcus Diener, apartment building, Güterstrasse, Basel, 1953

Marcus Diener, Le Building, location unknown, around 1960

Fellheimer, Wagner & Vollmer, Farragut Houses, New York, 1948–1950

Diener's first apartment house in the sense in which I am using the term here was the one built for the Migros pension fund in Basel's St. Johann district in 1951. Who lives in such apartments? Fortunately, there are directories that provide such information, street for street. The apartment house at Johanniterstrasse 15 is first mentioned in such a directory in 1953, when it is listed as having twenty single-room apartments spread over five stories. The twenty-one inhabitants are listed by name, first name, and occupation, telling us that nine were in commercial lines of work (clerk, secretary, or office assistant), three were laboratory technicians, and three were waitresses. The same picture emerges for the forty-eight single-room apartments at Johanniterstrasse 13. Along with other such occupations—businessman, sales assistant, clerk, short-hand typist, sales representative—the residents of these two apartment houses represent a cross-section of the urban class of salaried employees that Siegfried Kracauer described so tellingly in 1929.[23] Their homes may have been small—the main room was no more than 18 m² in size—but they lived within easy reach of restaurants, movie theaters (several built by Diener), and clubs.

Grossstadtarchitektur

Even allowing for the fact that their floor plans are almost certainly a direct outcome of the brief, these apartment houses and the history of this particular form of urban living warrant closer scrutiny. Ludwig Hilberseimer's *Grossstadtarchitektur* of 1927 includes a plan of a high-rise with apartments arranged along either side of a long corridor. Such apartment houses already existed in America, he wrote, citing as an example an apartment-hotel in Chicago, whose one-room apartments had a living room with breakfast room (i.e. a small kitchen) on one side and a dressing room on the other.[24] They were intended for permanent residence, Hilberseimer explained, and "in the future will doubtless become *the* big city form of dwelling."[25] By way of comparison, he also presented a floor plan of a two-room apartment very similar to those that Diener & Oberle built at Schützenmattstrasse 32–34.

Diener's draftsmen must have leafed through the Swiss magazines laid out in his office. A 1949 issue of *Bauen + Wohnen*, for example, featured the project of the Lake Shore Drive Apartments that Mies van der Rohe built in Chicago in 1947–1951.[26] One of those towers—Lake Shore Drive 880—contains eight 2.5-room apartments and the other four 4.5-room apartments per story, which in both cases are accessed via an inside corridor. But because these freestanding buildings are 20 m deep, the service areas—vestibule, kitchen, bathroom—can be lined up in a layer alongside the inside corridor, leaving the façade free for the living and sleeping area. In Diener's apartment houses, by contrast, the kitchen is almost always situated on the façade, if only to obviate the need for the expensive "mechanical ventilation systems" required by Canton Basel-Stadt's building regulations, the *Hochbautengesetz*.

Whether Diener's apartment houses can be read as evidence of a theoretical engagement with American urban housing is open to debate; but the office archives do contain a plan that looks conspicuously similar to a residential block in New York. Called simply "Le Building" and retroactively dated "ca. 1960," it features units whose layout is closely akin to that of the Farragut Houses that Fellheimer & Wagner and Vollmer built for the New York Housing Authority in Brooklyn, New York City, in 1948–1950. These star-shaped, thirteen- and fourteen-story blocks whose five tracts radiate out into the surrounding park were undoubtedly published in magazines like *Architectural Forum*. Who Diener's client was is not known, nor is the location for which the residential tower was intended. The Anglo-French name could indicate that the thirteen-story high-rise was for Toronto, where Marcus Diener also had an office for a while, and where in 1956–1960 he built two commercial buildings.[27]

Typological design

But is this quest for models for his apartment houses actually necessary? Might there not be purely pragmatic reasons for their typology, not least the technical, economic, and social factors governing the construction of new housing? This is actually the more likely hypothesis. The quality of the housing that Diener built in Basel in the 1950s is in any case attributable to something else. It attests to an approach to design that I would call "typological," in that it entails varying a given type according to the plot of land available, which is to be exploited to the full. This is especially evident in the structures built on very small plots, where small apartment houses were erected to replace older buildings. At Mittlere Strasse 67, for example, Diener interlocked the two 2-room apartments on each floor so that both would have a balcony facing the garden. These apartments, which he built on his own account, were renovated by Diener & Diener in 2014, when the kitchens were incorporated into the enlarged living rooms and the layouts thus "loosened up" in a way that Senn would have approved of.

The residential building at Schützenmattstrasse 32–34 dating from 1943 is 13 m deep, while that at Steinentorstrasse 14, built ten years later, is 15 m deep, permitting a typology of small apartments arranged on either side of an inside corridor. In the second case, the kitchenette and balcony are situated at the front, making for a modulated façade. One or two of Diener's freestanding buildings are even deeper and make full use of the 16 m maximum permitted by law. Here, the living room and bedroom are not arranged along the inside corridor, but instead are separated from it by a layer of service areas such as the bathroom, vestibule, and sometimes the kitchen, as at Lake Shore Drive 880. The finest example of this is without a doubt the apartment house at Auberg 3 in Basel, dating from 1959. This has eight single-room apartments per story, each of them with its own service area allocated to the room in the most ingenious way.

Most of these apartment houses were built by consortia founded by Diener with building contractors and were

---

Bild von kollektiven Wohnbauten am Beispiel des Apartmenthauses 'Dufour' in Basel," typescript, archive Roger Diener.
23 Siegfried Kracauer, *Die Angestellten aus dem neuesten Deutschland*, ext. sixth edition, Frankfurt am Main 1993 (first published Berlin 1930).
24 Ludwig Hilberseimer, *Grossstadtarchitektur*, Die Baubücher, vol. 3, Stuttgart 1927, pp. 18–19.
25 Hilberseimer 1927, (see note 24), p. 39.
26 Hugo Weber, "Mies van der Rohe in Chicago," in *Bauen + Wohnen*, vol. 1–5, no. 9 (1947–1949), pp. 1–12, p. 11.

27 The archives of Marcus Diener contain a floor plan labeled: "Le Building. Projet d'un immeuble collectif, 154 logements de 1-2-3 et 4 pièces plus cuisine, salle de bain, WC," as well as a perspective drawing and photograph of a model. The drawing bears a striking similarity to one by Fellheimer & Wagner for a star-shaped apartment block with six tracts.

later sold on the free market. The projects were shaped by economic considerations. The buildings had to have good mechanical systems and attractive entrances, hence the extensive use of polished marble cladding. They were, after all, the building's calling card, and consequently that of its residents, too. Yet much the same might be said of the projects for housing cooperatives, whose entrances—admittedly on a more modest scale—are typically articulated as a sandstone-clad niche, sometimes with an arched lintel and with a glazed front made of wood and aluminum.

From the 1940s to the 1960s

The architecture of Diener's projects for housing cooperatives is very much in line with general developments in the aftermath of World War II. Until the 1950s, these simple volumes have projecting roofs with cladding on the underside. The large, evenly spaced windows with three panes each in both living room and bedroom are fitted with shutters or roller shutters made of wood. The garden-side façades are modulated by the alternation of windows and deep-set balconies, whose masonry parapets project somewhat from the façade. It is a very simple architecture that lives from just a few structural details—and from that same composure that would later become a hallmark of the architecture of Diener & Diener. This is most painfully apparent where the shutters have been sacrificed to insulation, which by deepening the reveals has turned the windows into holes.

In the early 1950s, this attention to detail extended to other parts of the building, especially in the more middle-class residential buildings. The living-room window parapets from this period are sometimes ribbed—an element taken up recently by Diener & Diener—and sometimes articulated as railings in front of French windows. All in all, it is a friendly kind of architecture; but it remains matter-of-fact, even if the "little railings"—disparaged by Max Frisch as a "flight into the intimate"—are never lacking.[28] The façades gradually become more complex and begin to feature several different kinds of window, which together form a work of many parts as at Grenzacherstrasse 105 of 1955, where the balconies are made of iron and the parapets of Eternit. The detailing is pushed farthest in the apartment house at Steinentorstrasse 14, where ribbed bands, painted yellow, are offset against walls rendered in red. This is also the first instance of Diener's organization of the façade into horizontal bands—later a favorite, and often the only, design feature of a given building.

The late 1950s saw an architectural shift toward a resolutely cubic expression in which the edges of those residential buildings that end in an attic story are sometimes marked by a frame. Narrow balconies jut out from recesses in the façades, and the windows, interspersed with rectangles of render, form bands that are set back from the bands that form the parapets—and set apart from them in color, too, even if only slightly. The finest example of this radically simplified urban architecture is once again the freestanding apartment house with "flying" roof at Auberg 3 in Basel. And here, too, the encasing of the building in a layer of insulation has resulted in deep-set reveals, rendering an idiom that lives from its perfect proportioning of just a handful of elements banal. This is also the architecture that defines the residential buildings inserted into older rows, such as the apartment house at Solothurnerstrasse 50. At first glance ordinary, these buildings reveal their true qualities only on closer inspection—which is true of Diener's work in general.

By the 1960s, the parapets were made of concrete and more and more of them were being prefabricated, as were other elements, too. The façades became assemblages of such elements, even if by no means all of them were factory-made. The apartment block at Gundeldingerstrasse 57 is a good example of this. Prefabrication was now firmly on the agenda, both technically and architecturally, as is especially evident in two large developments or *grands ensembles* in Pratteln and Liestal, which belong to the third category of residential building in Diener's work. The typological thinking underpinning these large developments led to types that recall the debates of the 1920s, to floor plans that were used over and over again and to the extensive use of prefabricated elements. What we are talking about here in concrete terms are access-gallery floor plans such as those used by Walter Gropius on several occasions.

Prefabrication

The Weiermatt apartment blocks in Liestal that Diener built in 1967–1970 for a consortium of several company pension funds are a good example of his work of this period. The three slim high-rises, each twelve stories high, are positioned alongside, and at an angle to, a small river, one behind the other. Their typology matches that of the "slab buildings" that Gropius designed as examples for his research work on building "hoch, mittel oder flach?"[29] In contrast to those, however, the balconies here run across the full breadth of the façade. The construction is mixed. The prefabricated concrete elements are confined to the layer of galleries and balconies, while the windowless end façades are made of red brick. These elements had been developed earlier in the course of the studies undertaken for a different large development in Pratteln.[30] There, the windowless walls were clad in one-story-high concrete panels that resemble the parapets, thus giving the impression of a work of architecture made of a set of just a few prefabricated elements.

The aforementioned studies, which were done by a German engineer working in Diener's office, were part of a wider effort to build faster and more economically. In Switzerland this had begun in the 1950s in the French-speaking cantons, which had taken their cues from the French practice of *préfabrication lourde*. The company Industrie générale pour la construction (IGECO) was founded in Etoy, Canton Vaud, in 1957. Ernst Göhner would later buy into it so that he could have elements for his Göhnerswil projects produced in the works at

---

28 Max Frisch, "Cum grano salis," lecture transcript published in *Das Werk*, vol. 40, no. 10 (1953), pp. 325–329; on architecture after World War II, see also Martin Steinmann, "Auf der Suche nach einer Normalität," in *archithese*, no. 5 (1986): Um 1950 – Zürich und Kassel, pp. 15–23.

29 See Winfried Nerdinger, *Walter Gropius*, catalog for the exhibition at Busch-Reisinger-Museum, Harvard University Art Museums, Cambridge, MA; Bauhaus-Archiv, Berlin, Deutsches Architekturmuseum, Frankfurt am Main, Berlin 1985, pp. 136–139. The "slab buildings" were also published in English in Walter Gropius, *Scope of Total Architecture*, New York, 1955, pp. 103–15. These steel-frame high-rises never got off the drawing board, although Gropius frequently realized the same typology in his four- and five-story residential buildings.

30 According to Dieter Righetti, who joined Diener as an apprentice in 1961 and from 1964 worked on the Längi development in Pratteln. The responsible architect, a German engineer called Markus Rumpf, looked into the possibility of prefabricating elements in some depth.

Marcus Diener, apartment house, Auberg, Basel, 1959

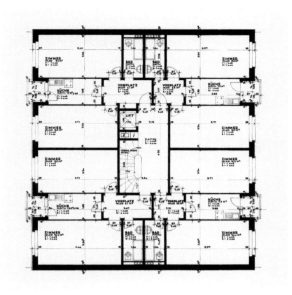
Marcus Diener, apartment building, Solothurnerstrasse, Basel, 1957

Marcus Diener, apartment house, Auberg, Basel, 1959

Marcus Diener, apartment house, Steinentorstrasse, Basel, 1953

Marcus Diener, high rise apartment buildings, Weiermatt, Liestal, 1967–1970

Marcus Diener, high rise apartment buildings, Weiermatt, Liestal, 1967–1970

Marcus Diener, Längi development, Pratteln, 1965–1970

Dom, Duret & Maurice, apartment building, Les Ailes, Cointrin, 1957–1959

Volketswil. The first residential building with elements prefabricated by IGECO, Les Ailes, was erected in Geneva in 1957–1959.[31] Contrary to what Larsen & Nielsen's license actually envisaged, however, its load-bearing parts are concrete frames, the façades are wood and Eternit panels.[32] This is noteworthy inasmuch as such prefabricated panels were developed for the Pratteln project, too—which makes perfectly good sense, since the balconies and galleries protect them from rain. According to Diener's own comparison of different types of construction, their use would save 1.836 m² of floor space per apartment. The panels were nevertheless abandoned in favor of more economical masonry—a fate that would befall prefabrication generally.

It is the structure of the posts, panels, and parapets that defines the look of Diener's residential buildings in Pratteln and Liestal. This is especially true of the side with the balconies. The variations in the spacing of the posts correspond to the division of the interior. Somewhat to our surprise, we discover that the more recent residential buildings by Diener & Diener, among them the long linear block Maaghof in Zurich-West, have returned to this elementary image. As to the grounds for such a limitation, we can do no more than speculate. Is the idea to concentrate the building's expressiveness in what few structural means it has at its disposal? It certainly makes for an expression of composure—the same composure, achieved with no more than windows and providing a backdrop for daily life in all its many manifestations, that characterizes the early developments of Marcus Diener.

Work in the office

Diener's residential buildings were shaped by their times, but also by the draftsmen who did the actual designing. These were technical draftsmen, which perhaps explains the pragmatic approach that defines all these buildings. With the possible exception of the apartment houses, there are no "inventions" among them. The floor plans are realizations of known types, according to the givens of the plot. As building method was clearly also a factor, the same details are repeated from one building to the next. The walls are made of brick that is 38 cm thick on the outside and 12 cm on the inside; the ceilings are 16-cm-thick concrete slabs with relatively short spans; and the interiors—the carpentry, i.e. doors, windows, closets etc.—are also standardized. Construction was thus fast and predictable.

In the 1960s, the procedure in the office was as follows: The designer in charge discussed the possibilities of a given plot with Marcus Diener and drew his design on a scale of 1:100. He then handed his drawings to the draftsmen, who working at their tilted drawing boards produced the working plans. The planning and site management were kept rigorously separate. Diener was no longer doing any designing himself by then, although he did make daily rounds of his draftsmen when he had the designer in charge update him on how the work was progressing.[33] His principal task was now to procure contracts, to which end he frequently founded the aforementioned consortia. Among Basel's architects, however, this earned him the reputation of being a property developer rather than an architect. That he and his office built large numbers of very simple, clear, and attractive residential buildings—and much else besides—is often overlooked. These buildings, moreover, offer a remarkably accurate gauge of the technical, economic, and social development of postwar architecture in Switzerland—at least to those willing to look long and hard enough.

---

31 Apartment block built by a cooperative of ground personnel working at Geneva airport, Les Ailes, in Geneva-Cointrin, architects Jean-Pierre Dom, Jean Duret, and François Maurice; see Dominique Zanghi, "Espoirs et aléas de la préfabrication en Suisse romande," in *matières* 3, 1999, pp. 86–95.
32 On the history of prefabrication in Switzerland generally, see Susanne Knopp and Markus Wassmer, "Der Reiz des Rationellen," in *Werk, Bauen + Wohnen*, vol. 82, no. 10 (1995), pp. 26–56.

33 According to Roger Diener and Dieter Righetti.

Housing—the Practice of Designing
A Conversation with Roger Diener

Roger Diener was interviewed by Martin Steinmann, Bruno Marchand and Alexandre Aviolat

Your first major projects after joining the office run by your father, Marcus Diener, were mostly housing projects, starting with the Hammerstrasse development (1978–1981). You soon positioned yourself as an architect heavily preoccupied with the typology of the dwelling and hence with the morphology of the city. This undoubtedly had to do with the contracts that the office was working on at the time. These projects nevertheless went far beyond just "doing your job" and give the impression of being more like research. What was the reason for this involvement in housing?

Housing is architecture's basic program. It's our job to build spaces for people, as manifested first and foremost in the dwelling. In the course of my professional life, I have seen that housing poses architecture's most fundamental question, which is how spaces can be organized for life. As limited as it may seem, it is actually the most complex and the most difficult program of them all. An office block is easier to organize than a residential building. In our work, it really is housing that raises the most questions and that prompts the most ideas regarding how we might answer them.

Theory

I've noticed in the office how much this program preoccupies us, far more than any other. It is the program that is most exciting and most interesting to work on. Thinking about the theoretical writings on architecture that really matter to me, they all concern housing—like the essay in which Walter Benjamin distinguishes between the two different ways of appropriating things: by use and by perception. The first of these, he writes, is accomplished "in a state of distraction," which is to say by habit. This form of appropriation is especially apparent in housing.

In 1926 Adolf Behne published a book in which he drew a very clear distinction between rationalism and functionalism in modern architecture; the former seeks general solutions, he wrote, and the latter solutions that are tailored to a specific task. Where does your architecture stand in relation to these two tendencies?

I called the talk I gave at the Department of Architecture at the ETH Lausanne in 1984 "Mach' die Kiste nicht zu klein" (lit. "Don't make the box too small"), which is the remark that Mies van der Rohe famously made to Hugo Häring, with whom he was sharing an office at the time. Häring was a proponent of functionalism in Behne's sense of the word. What Mies van der Rohe was saying was that spaces should not be shaped solely by their intended function, which is precisely the position that Behne in his book describes as rationalism. As functions change, we have to define them broadly enough to allow for such changes, because "the rationalist thinks in the long term." These comments have remained as relevant as ever for me and they are still eminently suited to bringing clarity to the debate about architecture generally and housing especially, and to drawing conclusions for design. But we also have to recognize that in this postmodernist age of ours, it is no longer a question of coming down on the side of one or other of these concepts, which Behne doesn't do either, by the way. He simply identifies two tendencies, which he then proceeds to describe.

"Organic" architecture

The development we were thinking of when we asked that question was the interest shown by recent Swiss architecture in concepts that share certain characteristics with functionalism, even if they actually rest on a very different premise. They might be called "organic" inasmuch as the floor plans that they produce dispense with right angles. They seem rather to be adapted to free movement through the dwelling—to taking a stroll through the rooms, as it were.

There are two reasons for such floor plans, which incidentally might also be described as "expressive functionalism," inasmuch as the dwelling is conceived as an expression of the specific use of its spaces. The first reason is economic in nature and results from the fact that apartments in Switzerland are larger than elsewhere, which gives architects more scope when designing their spaces. The second reason is cultural. The *salon*, or living room, long a middle-class privilege, is increasingly being called into question on the scale of the "normal" apartment of today. These days the kitchen is frequently incorporated into the space that used to be the living room, which consequently has become more of a multipurpose space. That used to be unthinkable. I remember how in my childhood, one typical feature of a working-class home was that the cooking was also done in the main room.

The petrified floor plan

The blurring of the boundaries between the various functions gives rise to new spatial options. The corridor between the daytime and nighttime rooms, for example, can be abandoned, which is what we did for the first time with the Warteckhof apartments (1992–1996), although we did provide a movable closet that might serve this function. Not only does the closet add definition to the large space, but it also shields the doors to the bedrooms. This "hall" has to provide space for various activities that generally take place separately—which is what makes it so interesting.

My reservation about the apartments that you're talking about does not concern their open geometry, which after all can be enriching, but rather those floor plans in which combining functions does *not* make for a freer use of the spaces after all. Taking advantage of this geometry for the composition of an apartment does not of itself make it interesting, at least not to me; it is interesting only if it opens up new functional possibilities. Often, however, these floor plans have a limiting impact on how the rooms are used. This also has to do with the fact that the circulation areas are now part of the individual rooms—unlike in older apartments, where the rooms are accessed from a corridor, or from each other if there are connecting doors. On entering a room, therefore, you have the whole room at your disposal, whereas rooms that have to double as passages are much harder to furnish ...

I know one of the apartments built by EMI Architekten in Zurich-Hottingen. It's a very nice apartment, but I can't imagine using the rooms in any way other than the way the current inhabitants use them. There simply *is* nowhere else to put the table. Here, you have to submit to the dictates of the rooms.

And another thing: These "organic" floor plans are rarely realized in a way that allows them to change shape in practice. These are not the free floor plans of the kind postulated by Le Corbusier. In the *plan libre*, the load-bearing and partitioning structures are kept separate and spaces can be combined to allow the apartment to be used in new ways. That's not the case with the floor plans we're talking about here. The rooms seem to derive their shape from their use, and in truth are like film stills that freeze-frame the lives being led inside them ...

... as in the fairytale of Sleeping Beauty!

Except that I'm not sure how such spaces might be "kissed back to life"!

Innovation

Some architects have become hooked on the idea that dwelling has changed fundamentally compared with what it used to be, and that there is therefore a need for innovation in the design of new housing.

That is certainly borne out by several different residential buildings built in Switzerland for progressive cooperatives over the past twenty years. Most were conceived for new forms of cohabitation. But even for a program like that, we would still endeavor to increase the potential uses to which the rooms can be put. We tried to put this into practice even in the large apartments of the Hammerstrasse development.

We also try to adapt the customary floor plans in our small apartments, too. A three-room apartment in Paris-Billancourt (2005–2009) has 65 m² of floor space on average, sometimes a little more. The conditions prevailing there are thus very different from those in Zurich-Affoltern, say, where such an apartment has 80 to 90 m². That greatly limits the scope for invention! In this situation, the organization of some of the more recent hotel rooms points up one possible avenue of innovation, if you want to call it that: You can incorporate the bathroom into the room—as is done sometimes—or at least furnish it with an inside window to let in some daylight. This is also true of other rooms. When renovating a residential building on Voltastrasse in Basel 2009, for example, we combined the bathroom and kitchen in a single room, which can be partitioned as and when necessary. The sink is like a washbasin. Our aim was to make these rooms bigger ...

... so you wash in the kitchen, just like in the tenements of the nineteenth century.

It's interesting to imagine abandoning dedicated rooms for the sake of making the dwelling as a whole more accommodating of several different uses, in other words for the sake of making it perform better.

Most rooms are allocated specific uses alone on grounds of size—the square meters determine how they are used. If that kind of dedication of space is abandoned, it will have consequences for the rooms, which will become more equal. But to return to your example: Incorporating the kitchen may make the living room larger, but it also allows its floor area to be reduced. And this brings us back to Gropius's observation that people actually need very little space, especially if that space is well furnished from the "operational" point of view, in other words, pared down to a "minimum dwelling." The innovation back then consisted in viewing the dwelling in economic terms.

If you think of the apartments of the late nineteenth century and of the "stone city," such an apartment signified a major cultural step forward. With the larger apartments of today we have some interesting possibilities that Gropius couldn't even have imagined. Take what Lacaton Vassal have done to those little apartments in Bordeaux, for example. They've essentially fronted the rooms with a deep, glazed space across the full breadth of the apartment and hence at the same time reorganized it. This kind of manipulation seems very interesting to me, even if we take a different path.

As far as the form of the apartments is concerned, we must first talk about the new social givens. If you're talking about homes for singles—for example for elderly people who are to be offered a different way of living—then the innovations have a serious side to them. Take the apartments being built on the Hunziker Areal in Zurich. These are essentially clusters of small living rooms and bedrooms in between communal spaces. If these give rise to more complex spatial layouts that we feel to be "organic," then that is certainly an interesting development.

The rooms in your projects are at the inhabitants' disposal, as it were; they can do what they like with them. In more recent apartments, on the other hand, inhabitants often have difficulty accommodating the simplest of things.

In the late 1980s, Gilles Barbey and I did a research project at the EPFL on how people furnish their apartments. We worked with students on the relationships that existed between the apartments in Lausanne's Tunnel district and the residents who lived in them. They didn't speak of spaces as such, but rather of this or that window, the railing in front of it, the radiator below it, if there was one at all … Their perception of the rooms had little to do with their composition, but was more concerned with individual elements—and in the Tunnel district with the location, too, starting with the view out of the window. We were impressed how charged with meaning the rooms were for their occupants.

Comparing those with the kind of abstract rooms that magazines are so fond of publishing, I get the impression that their inhabitants can actually set up very little—just a few things, carefully arranged, as there is no room for anything else. That's not enough for me. I think an apartment should offer space for those personal things with which its inhabitants want to surround themselves.

Limited means

The rationalization of building meant that dwellings built after World War II, if not before, had to forfeit their crafted interiors. What woodwork there is, is now confined to doors and windows, and perhaps a windowsill. And even these parts are no longer the work of craftsmen. This has made interiors abstract, and I doubt that white, free-form rooms have the capacity to compensate for the loss of the woodwork that used to be universal, even in humble interiors. Think of paneling, for instance. Perhaps some other materials and methods that are still available today—wallpaper, for instance—might have more success. But it seems to me that a room cannot compensate for the reduction of details to which Modernism has subjected it through expressive form alone. No, we should rather be questioning the abstract room itself, even in orthogonal spaces.

Types

For several centuries housing's limited repertoire of floor plans was taken for granted. These were adapted to the prevailing conditions, meaning that the type was realized from case to case. What interests us about the work of Diener & Diener is an approach to design that belongs to this conception of housing. The Warteck Plan is a case in point. It raises the question: How do you proceed when you get down to work? What makes you choose one type over another?

We have these types in our heads and review case by case how appropriate are the ideas to which they give form. One question that arises for us is the permeability of the apartment. Is this to be accomplished by opening a bedroom to the living room so that together they form a whole? That can be done with double doors, for example, which is something we often make use of. In the Warteckhof, for example, we have the living room facing one way only, but put the doors to the bedrooms next to each other so that they form a kind of counterweight to the living room.

The question of permeability has to do with the place and how it is to be experienced spatially. Is the living area to face two ways at once? Or are we going to say: it's actually very nice to have a living room facing onto the courtyard alone—in which case, we can confine it to the rear. As I see it, the question of the spatial perceptions created by the various types comes right at the start of our work. What do we want? What do we not want? And then we have the external conditions: How deep is the floor plan? Is the bathroom inside or outside, that is to say, on the façade? Where is the staircase? How is the neighborhood?

The type with the through living room that we used in Wallisellen (2008–2014) needs a lot of space and hence comes up only once or twice in our projects. Things look rather different when part of it takes the form of a *Wohnküche*, or eat-in kitchen. That's basically a nostalgic floor plan—namely the floor plan that Göhner used in his developments. The kitchen either has a glazed door that lets in light from the "other" side or it can be left open to create a contiguous space. That is a type that we have often used in our more recent projects.

We call it the "Göhner Plan."
The through living room with integrated kitchen and dining area is very common in contemporary housing. The great advantage of it is that it lends itself to diverse urban situations. And you can have the sunlight come in at either end, which makes it an especially good solution for developments with a central courtyard, like in Wallisellen.
If we study Diener & Diener's floor plans, we notice that the types are inflected according to the cultural conditions prevailing in a given place, that is, according to the habits of the people who live there. The realization of the Warteck Plan in Ypenburg (2000–2003), for example, has the kitchen behind the living room, and hence in the dark, rather than alongside it as it is in Basel. And it is open, too, which perhaps is more in line with Dutch habits.

The kitchen is open in Basel, too, and connected to the living room by a 2-m-wide opening. But there are indeed cultural differences that determine how a type is actually realized. Such differences can exist within one and the same city, however. Take the question of how you enter an apartment. In the residential building on the Warteck Areal in Basel there is a small vestibule, whereas in a different residential building of the same type (1992–1996), also in Basel, you step straight into the living room. We proposed a closet that would have created a kind of vestibule—as we did for the Warteckhof—but in the end decided to leave it up to the tenants. It's not just a question of habit; it's also about space, since without the closet, the living room is larger. So you have to decide. I personally would not want a closet there, even if it's more genteel to have a kind of vestibule. What counts is that the tenant can make a choice.

Objectivity

You've said on various occasions that your housing does not tell any stories. Can this be understood as relating to your floor plans? After all, you're not going to amaze anybody if you work with a limited number of types as those types are familiar. Is this a search for objectivity?

I can't lay claim to objective values for our work. But it's true: underlying what we're discussing here is the search for something like that, as opposed to the subjective values that I see in "organic" floor plans. This is not a value judgment, however, and I'm not saying that our stance is better than any other; I'm saying only that we like to have objectivity in our architecture.

Coming back to the two positions that Behne described, the distinction he drew between rationalism and functionalism, presumably you would opt for the first of these: for the creation of spaces that people can appropriate as they wish and that allow for developments in their way of life over time. Even if Behne tended toward rationalism, he was nevertheless fascinated by functionalism, by the adaptation of architecture to a given purpose.

If we're talking about "normal" apartments, then the two positions in fact collide. To understand this, you have only to compare the residential buildings of Gropius and Häring in the Berlin-Siemensstadt development. Their floor plans are practically identical; where they differ is in the façades. The differences became more pronounced after the war, as in the Romeo and Julia high-rises that Hans Scharoun built in Stuttgart, although their *raison d'être* was spatial rather than functional in nature.

You spoke earlier of your efforts to lend spaces certain qualities, even on the fringes of social housing. Were you talking about the dimensions and proportions of these spaces?

We work first and foremost on a good ceiling height, which is something we really fight for. We think it makes a huge difference whether a ceiling is 2.4 or 2.6 or even 2.7 meters high. We also work on elements such as doors and windows. We use windows made of wood on the inside—in other words wood and aluminum windows—and then doors made of wood as a way of generating a relationship between these elements. Admittedly, we sometimes achieve very little by this. In the Markthallen Tower for example (2007–2012), we used different kinds of wood for the doors to the apartments believing that it would give each of them its own distinct identity ... It actually makes a somewhat informal impression.

Materials

I'd like to move on to a different matter, namely the materials that define how your buildings look, in other words, the materialization of the façades, which for a long time were either concrete or brick. What motivates your choice of material? Is it the place? In Meggen, for instance, you've built two houses made of wood standing in an old park (2006–2012).

Constructing small houses out of stone is something I find very, very demanding. There are only a few really good examples, in part owing to the building regulations, which require an attic floor. We look long and hard for our materials. In St. Alban-Tal in Basel (1984–1986), for example, we used wood for the rear of one of the buildings because of the old craft shops there.

So the larger context defines the materials used?

Well, the wood used in Champfèr (2008–2015) was not dictated by the place, as the typical Engadine house is made of stone with white render. So if the larger context was referenced at all, then only by the color. No, the question is more complex than that. Rendered façades are the most demanding as they leave only a few windows with which to make "architecture." So there's something abstract about such façades—just think of the Wittgenstein House, for example. Façades made of wood, by contrast, have something concrete about them. They tend to soften the clear-cut look of the volume.

Is this because of the "assembled" look of such a façade, because you can still see the individual boards, even where they've been painted over?

Yes, that's probably true. The dimensions of the elements available result in a pleasingly structured skin. Take the strips covering the joints between the boards in St. Alban-Tal, for example. They show how the outer shell was made, so you don't have that uneasy feeling of not knowing what is concealed beneath it. Viewed in this way, our use of wood in the more recent projects has brought relief. But obviously it still depends on the place. The two buildings in Meggen blend in with the humble old houses already there, even if they're larger. And their cladding harmonizes better with them than the rendered houses that are there, too.

Your use of wood in your more recent buildings has not been confined to the skin alone—not least on account of a change in the building regulations.

And the zeitgeist! Our experience with this material in the 1980s was twofold: We'd wanted to build the Galerie Gmurzynska in Cologne entirely out of wood, but the insurers said no and the fire safety certificate was impossible to come by, leaving us with no choice but to content ourselves with wood cladding.

So the cladding material became a statement. These days that's the norm, as the façade is in any case broken down into layers: the load-bearing layer made of concrete, the insulation, the cladding made of sheet metal, wood, brick, or rather facing brick applied vertically so that we can see that they're stuck on, as in your Maaghof building in Zurich-West (2002–2013). Because of the energy specifications, the skin is actually no more than decoration, although it can still reference the larger context. Façades no longer have to be made of brick in order to say: "This used to be an industrial site."

That is certainly true, although we feel ourselves to be on surer ground if the load-bearing structure is also made of wood rather than just the cladding, as is often the case these days. The structural conditions change very little, the spans for sure, although in housing the spans are in any case limited, which is why wood is also a suitable material. We're currently building a seven-story block in Lyon (2016–2020) that is made entirely of wood. The deep balconies are nevertheless supported by pillars made of concrete. The use of wood was a condition, only you don't see it, because according to the authorities, above all the *maire*, "there's no visible wood in Lyon."

Ornament

The boards of the parapets on the residential building in Meggen are arranged so that they have an ornamental impact. To speak more generally, it seems the parapets in your more recent projects have taken on the function of an ornament that has the effect of loosening up an otherwise rather

> *severe architecture. It starts with Maaghof, where they look as if they were made of round bricks, but in fact are made of concrete. What motivated this look—which after all is what it is, an image?*

What counts for us is the experience the ornament evokes. This kind of openwork wall made of round bricks is familiar to us from villas by Schinkel or from the country estates in Italy that inspired him. So the motivation was the "yearning for the south," which is a yearning that is always there for me—as evidenced just recently by the terrace on top of the Ferrari dealership in Basel (2017).

The starting point for the design, however, is not so much the delight in ornament. Pickets alone are not enough to define the façade of a residential building. If the balconies are not to look like holes, then we design parapets to prevent it. It's less about the pleasure we take in an ornamental effect than our interest in a façade that clearly delimits space. We try to articulate the parapet in such a way that even if it is permeable, it still defines a space. That is our starting point in most cases. It's curious, but pickets in modern architecture never really bothered me because there they look good—and sophisticated. But the way they're used today I find paltry and unimaginative in most instances. I don't know why that is either.

> *In his famous lecture "Cum grano salis" of 1953, Max Frisch made fun of the "little railings" of the housing developments being built at the time. In plain, objective architecture, these are indeed the places where the need for beauty is indulged. They are a good way of relativizing rather severe-looking façades . . .*

. . . or of activating them. Often what is lacking to mediate between building and person is some point of detail. That is what such parapets do.

> *The problem of the parapets comes up wherever your residential buildings have through balconies, which is almost always the case. What is the reason for this form?*

It has to do with how we experience the outside. It is definitely an upgrade for an apartment if the balconies are not just stuck-on boxes or cages. Stepping outside should broaden your horizons, but it should also hold your gaze. Parapets of the kind that we design are intended to prevent it from going astray. Being permeable, they define the dividing line between inside and outside. Thanks to the parapet, the balcony is part of the apartment.

Work with artists

> *The parapets for the building in Paris-Billancourt were designed by Peter Suter. You often work with artists on your projects.*

The first time we did so was the project for two residential buildings on the Rue de la Roquette in Paris (1992–1996), for which Dani Karavan put a poem on the wall closing off the courtyard—and planted a tree, too. You have to find artists who are interested in this kind of collaboration. Josef Felix Müller develops his ideas by discussing them with us. I invited Müller to create a frieze for the façade above the stores in Wallisellen. He executed it as a dry-stone wall, which was a play on the formerly rural character of the place.

We have an intimation, a notion, of what the outcome of the collaboration will be. For the Swiss Embassy in Berlin (1995–2000), for example, our drawings of the large firewall resembled those that Helmut Federle then developed. The work of an artist gives us an idea, and we then invite him or her to work with us, without knowing exactly what the outcome will be. But we always have an idea; we don't invite an artist to do just anything. In the case of the residential buildings in Champfèr it was all about the wood cladding. The ornaments that Müller had cut in the boards resemble forms by Hans Arp or the "drawings" of a bark beetle.

> *Your architecture is sometimes described as intentionally banal. I'm not blameless here, as I once titled an essay about the office building on Hochstrasse (1985–1988) "Le sens du banal." You can do that in French; but in English the word is disparaging.*

Architecture *for* the city

In architecture there have to be parts that go unnoticed, that are not even supposed to be noticed. Adopting Benjamin's distinction, those are the parts that we appropriate by use, not by perception. This has nothing to do with banality in the pejorative sense of the word. The word is wrong for a different reason, too. If we work on these parts, if we define their proportions, then they will be just as relevant to the whole as those parts that we endow with a specific look—for example the parapets we were talking about just now. Without a background, they would not stand out. Both elements are always present in our projects. Architecture only really becomes banal when everything remains on the level of the parts that go unnoticed, and whose monotony is not a feature, as it is with Luigi Snozzi, say—which probably works in his case. But it has very little to do with architecture if everything goes unnoticed.

> *You spoke earlier of those flat façades whose architecture consists in the proportions of the windows. Diener & Diener were for a long time famous for such façades. Other concepts arose later on. In the housing projects in Amsterdam (1995–2001) and Berlin (1994–2000), for example, it is the grids that divide up the façades; in more recent projects, like Wallisellen (2008–2014) and Bülach (2013–2019), it is the pilasters between the windows.*

The pilasters lend the façades a certain depth through "le jeu savant . . ."—through the play of light that they evoke. They give the wall an impact like waves, which in a way is like the corrugated glazing of the Swiss Re building (2008–2017). The effect is striking. It directs the perception to the wall itself, which no longer looks like a skin, but is the wall itself. We perceive it as something in its own right. And another thing: the pilasters take the edge off the proportions that used to define our façades, making them rather less acute. To quote Roland Barthes, the proportions are no longer the *punctum* of the façade—the thing that demands our attention, in other words. That is not harmless, but if all goes well, the pilasters lend the façade a new quality that amounts to more than just the relationship between the openings.

There are two sides to this, both of which fascinate me in equal measure. On the one hand it has something of classical architecture about it, while on the other, it is what John Ruskin called "mere building" of the kind familiar to us from nineteenth-century factory buildings. These façades have both.

What all your projects have in common is a certain composure; they speak for themselves. You refrain from the kind of architecture that is not rooted in the materials out of which it is built.

We live in an age in which pretty much anything an architect gets into his head can in fact be built. I'm thinking here of Jean Nouvel's new apartment block in Lyon. The whole regularity and the whole solidity of that district dating back to the nineteenth century is now having to make way for "innovation." The technical and economic givens of the age were of course essential to the achievement of that regularity, but for architects who want to attract notice through their buildings, everything is possible. In this situation I'm often reminded of an important lecture that Bernard Huet gave in Lausanne called "L'architecture contre la ville."

Huet's contention was that art rebelled against convention and that as long as architecture defined itself as an art, it was bound to rebel against the city that as a collective work stood for convention. Some architects create "innovative" buildings as a way of doing a bit of art. In one of your own lectures you took a stand against this determination to renew architecture at all costs.

You can't be opposed to innovation per se; that would be reactionary. To create spaces that we have not yet experienced seems to me to be a legitimate aspiration, at least on the face of it. The real question is to what extent we can abstract from the conditions that gave rise to this or that convention. Have the inhabitants changed? Have their habits changed? I'm often amazed at how fascinated people are by dwellings that are "different," but highly impractical and at how willing they are to put up with that. It is as if the "novelty" of their dwellings had an intoxicating effect on them.

But the question of innovation is mainly of concern to architects, I think. Whether or not a property venture is a success does not depend on the things we're talking about here. All the units in Paris-Billancourt were sold for 10,000 euros per square meter even before the construction site had been set up. The same thing happened in Lyon for 6,000 euros per square meter. People are interested in the size of the apartment and in the kitchen equipment, but otherwise ...

And they are also interested in the location, the neighborhood, the services, the public transport, in short the infrastructure.

Yes, the location is often more important than the architecture, and I think people are right to be demanding on that point.

The situation of the architect

I have one last question in this connection. Since those first projects in Basel, you've built numerous residential buildings in Switzerland, Austria, Germany, Holland, Belgium, France, Italy ... And you've planned just as many others that never got off the drawing board. How has the status of the architect on the housing market changed over this long period?

The projects have become denser and have higher occupancy rates; but above all, the promoters loom much larger than they used to, and they pay much closer attention to the returns. There's nothing wrong with that as long the optimization that we are to be part of is transparent. Unfortunately that's not always the case. Then there's another development: the people you deal with in the course of a project tend to change. At first, you and the developer's representatives at least share the experience of the competition and this generates trust when you go on to manage the project together. But sooner or later, the developer's people move on and are replaced by others who are not bound to you by that shared experience. And that makes our work more difficult.

In other words, the conditions governing new housing have become more difficult since the 1970s and your first two projects?

They most certainly have! But even if the conditions demand more of us than they used to, they do not prevent us from seeking—and finding—good solutions. As I said at the beginning of our conversation, housing is still the task that interests me most in practice.

Buildings and Projects
1978–2020

Hammerstrasse

Apartment Buildings, Basel, Switzerland, 1978–1981

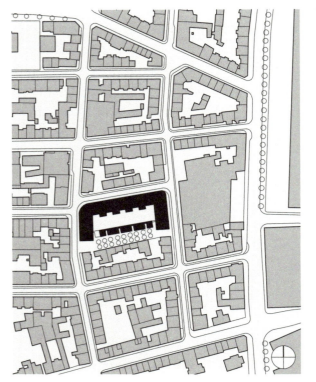

The former industrial zone is located in the densely populated Matthäus district. It occupies approximately half of a city block. The new apartment buildings complete the existing block perimeter development. In this way, Diener & Diener responded to ongoing discussions concerning the "architecture of the city." The project combines traits of "stone city" of late nineteenth-century urbanism, so characteristic of this neighborhood, with the qualities of early-twentieth-century "green city." This accounts for the considerable attention received by the project when under development.

Significant as well is the close proximity of residential and productive activities, itself treated here as an urbanistic form. In a way analogous with the traditional perimeter block development, with apartment buildings facing the street and commercial structures on the interior, a row of two-story studio buildings closes off the new, green courtyard. Traversing the block as a whole is an alleyway, which leads past the new studios and the old commercial buildings.

The development consists of three tracts which contain diversified apartments. On Bläsiring, the bedrooms are oriented toward the street, while the living rooms—with their large windows and verandas—face the courtyard. On the two short tracts, the bedrooms face either the street or the courtyard, and open onto a large, centrally positioned living area. This arrangement represents an attempt to create apartments whose utilization is more open-ended than is customary. Among other things, they were conceived for apartment-sharing communities.

The architectonic language articulates an opposition between street and courtyard. The street façade display a grooved pedestal of the kind often found in the quarter. The pedestal zone is two-storied, and consists of prefabricated concrete panels. Rising above this level are whitewashed brick walls. The uniformly configured windows are square, and have cruciform subdivisions. The courtyard façade are given ribbon windows. The verandas on the long tract are in metal and glass. They are carried by delicate, two-storied supports and provide a setting for daily affairs. The two corners of the block which face the street are glazed; with their expressive design, they recall Constructivist buildings of the 1920s.

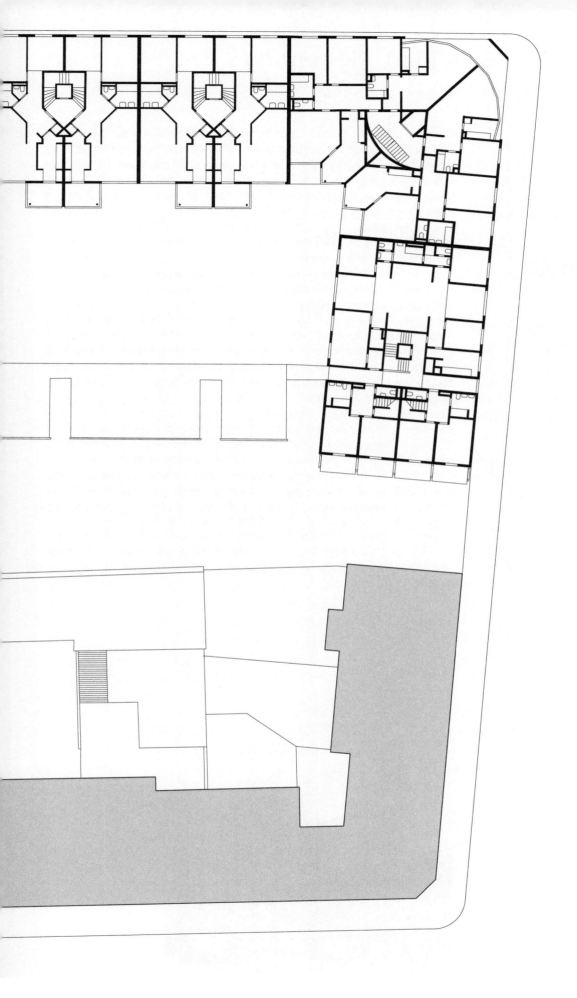

Apartment and Office Buildings, Riehenring

Apartment and Office Buildings, Basel, Switzerland, 1980–1985

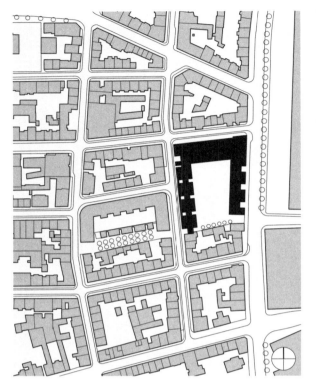

The development combines residential and commercial uses. It forms the perimeter of a large site which adjoins the apartment buildings on Hammerstrasse. Here as well as there, it was a question of integrating the design into a partially pre-existing street block. For Diener & Diener, the street block serves as a conceptual matrix. Through a *recherche patiente*, it allows them to investigate the relationship between morphological and typological orders. The apartments are supplemented by commercial spaces. The Migros shop in particular allows the development to play the role of a center for the neighborhood.

Residential and commercial buildings form a large courtyard, which was initially accessible to the public. The appearance of the development results from a collage of diverse typologies. In contradistinction to the earlier development, the various parts are not unified through a shared architectonic language; instead, each is recognizable in its typological particularity. Preserved meanwhile is the urbanistic hierarchy. Living areas are oriented toward the street, with bedrooms—all of them identical—facing the spacious, treed courtyard. The continuous balconies, on the other hand, are detached from this hierarchy: in the wing on Riehenring, they are set along the courtyard in front of the bedrooms. In the other wing, they are situated in front of the living areas, along Efringerstrasse. The roof of the apartment building on Riehenring is formed as a terrace with swimming pool. A narrow staircase leads from the balconies to the roof.

The industrial materials employed—a nod to the earlier industrial utilization of the site—do not reference the primarily residential character of the development. The façade designs are varied: on the one hand, they serve to indicate the respective utilization; on the other, they serve to differentiate the sections. The façades are masonry, either plastered in white or clad in white enameled corrugated sheet metal with the exception of the façade on Riehenring, which consists of horizontally mounted Profilit.

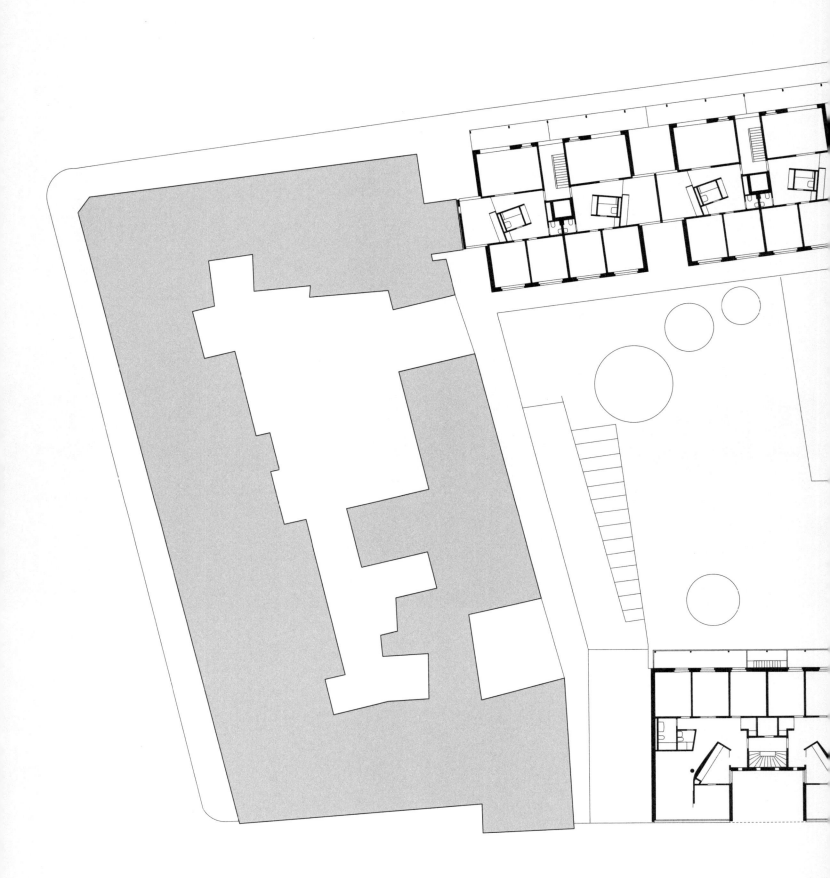

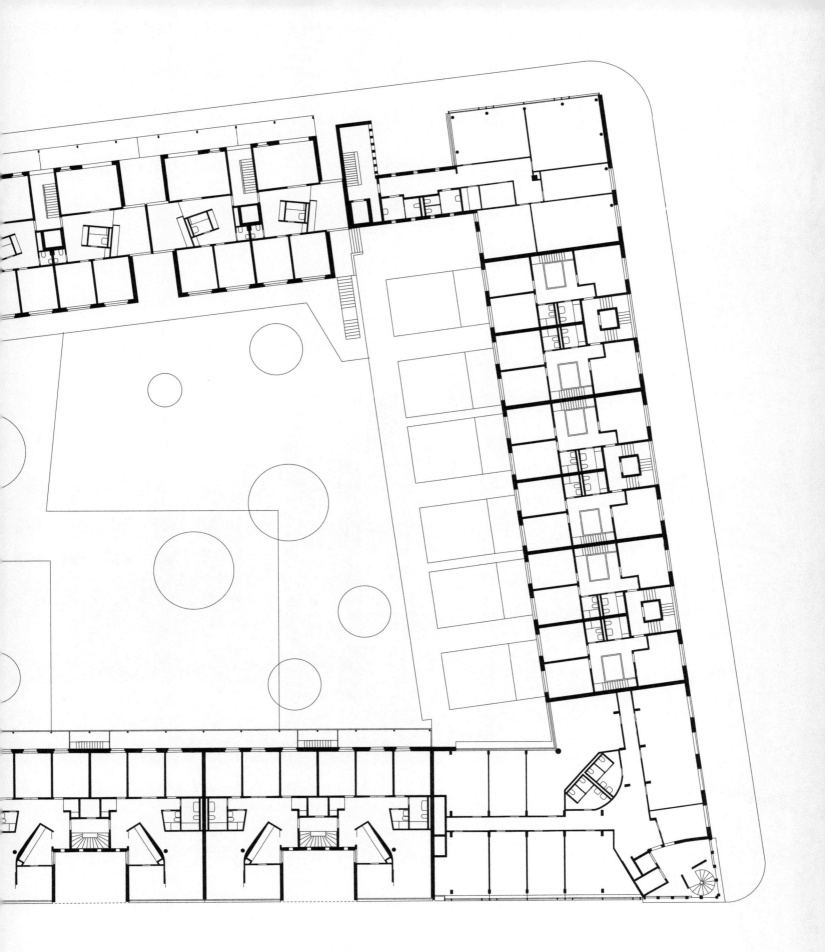

St. Alban-Tal

Apartment Buildings, Basel, Switzerland, 1981–1986

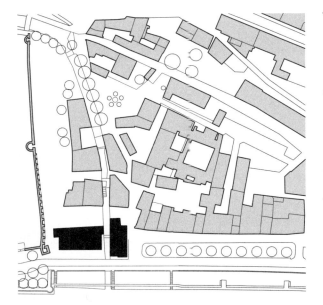

The design emerged from a competition Diener & Diener won in 1981. It comprises two apartment buildings in St. Alban-Tal, a historic commercial area serviced by a canal. They stand on the former site of two long-since demolished paper mills. One of the buildings is set parallel to the canal, the other parallel to the Rhine River, and set back somewhat from the promenade that runs along it.

The building to the east has four stories; it is not far from the city wall, and is an element of the promenade prospect. Each floor has two large apartments. The typology consists of three layers: facing the Rhine are the living rooms and kitchens, which are connected along the windows to form open spatial structures; toward the neighborhood the bedrooms form a cell structure. Set between the two are the corridors and wet rooms. The walls that define the layers form load-bearing structures.

The apartment building to the west has three stories and consists of two layers. Its load-bearing structure is formed as a prop grid. The bedrooms lying along the canal and the wet rooms correspond to this grid, while the living rooms and kitchens set along the square are independent of it, having free floor plans. Their façades are set in front of the supports, and are not load-bearing.

In both buildings, the configuration of the apartments displays a clear differentiation between front and back, as expressed by the façades. The architecture conforms to the principle of the connection of fragments. The white plastered front of the apartment building to the east contrasts with the rear façade, clad in wood, while the rear of the apartment building to the west, which takes the form of a glazed grid, is distinct from the front façade, also in white plaster. In this way, the architecture responds to essential traits of the neighborhood including Roland Rohn's buildings for Hoffmann-La Roche on the opposite bank of the Rhine.

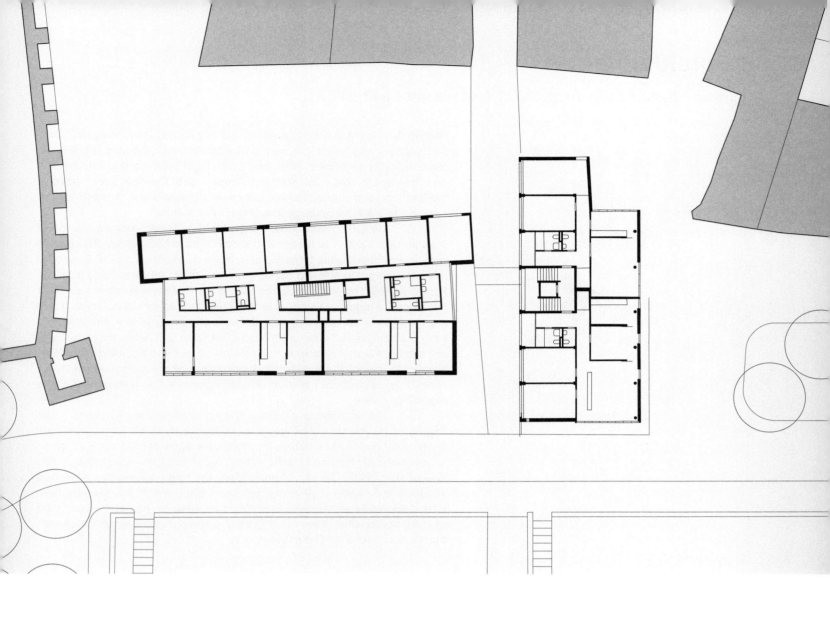

Burgfelderplatz

Apartment Building with Bank, Basel, Switzerland, 1982–1985

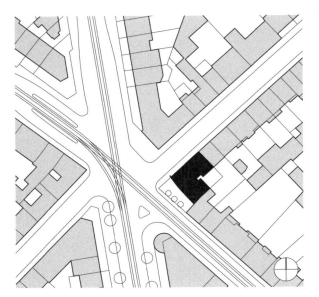

This small residential and commercial building stands at a heavily trafficked intersection, and forms one corner of a street block. On Missionsstrasse, the building is set back in conformity with legal building line. This creates an urban space that is planted with three trees. The two street sides of the building are distinguished markedly through their façades, which respond to the surroundings in architectonic terms.

On Missionsstrasse, the building accommodates a branch of the Cantonal Bank. The corner entrance is clad in black stone. The bank's name—which is visible from the distance—is inscribed on the firewall of the neighboring apartment building, in French for those arriving from the French border. The entrance to the apartments is on a side street alongside the display windows of a shop. In the upper stories, groups of three apartment units are clustered around a single staircase, which is illuminated from the courtyard. These units have either 3 or 1.5 rooms in the customary arrangement: living rooms and kitchens oriented toward the street, bedrooms toward the courtyard at the corner of the parcel. In the living areas, long cupboards partition off a corridor, creating a threshold to the nighttime zones.

The architecture follows the principle of an expressive interlinking of fragments. The façade on Missionsstrasse is slightly curved; by virtue of their sense of flow, the ribbon windows of the verandas, given an emphatically horizontal articulation, recall the Expressionist architecture of the 1920s. On St. Johanns-Ring, the large, uniformly configured windows are nearly square, and are given a cruciform subdivision; their form does not reveal the utilization of the rooms. In the narrow courtyard the bedrooms, which have French doors, open onto narrow balconies with parapets consisting of iron tubing.

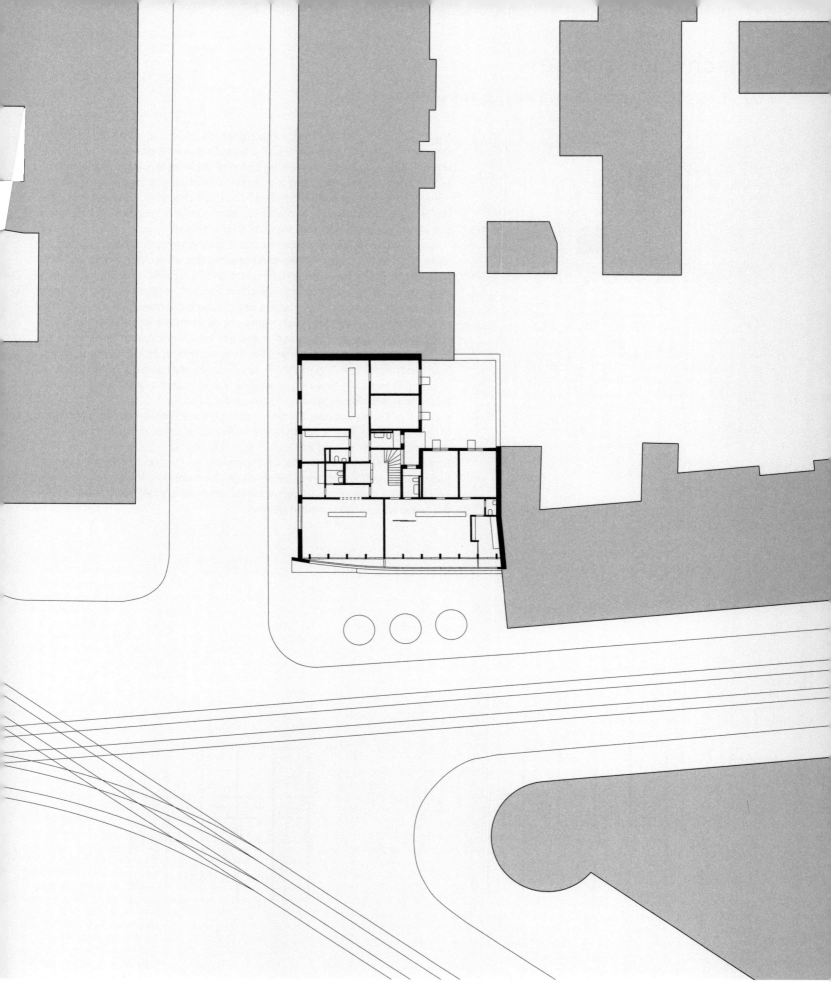

Allschwilerstrasse

Apartment Building, Basel, Switzerland, 1984–1986

The building stands alongside the trench of the railway line that passes through this city toward France. It is attached to an older apartment building, and occupies nearly the entire parcel. Following the angle of the trench on the outside of the building is a continuous staircase that leads from the garden to an acute-angled terrace in the fourth story. Throughout its entire height, the staircase is clad in a concrete latticework which shapes the windowless façade that faces the railway line.

The building combines two highly divergent typologies. In the lower three stories above the pedestal zone, there is an apartment on each side of the staircase, which is situated on the façade. The balconies run along the apartments' entire breadths. In conformity with the western boundary of the parcel, the glazing behind the balconies is slightly oblique in relation to the façade, which produces an unstable impression from the outside. The apartments above these are two-storied, and are accessed in two ways via an inner corridor. Like bridges, they span the corridor, which leads to the terrace. Serving them as a balcony is a narrow, projecting strip. In compliance with building regulations, the upper stories are recessed laterally somewhat in relation to those below.

On the façade, the two typologies are displayed as contrasting architectonic registers, so that the building looks as though it were produced by stacking two different volumes, one on top of the other. The horizontal perforations of the balconies below contrast with the vertical, two-story windows above. The construction consists of simple materials, and is partly concrete and partly plastered masonry; all parts—excluding the latticework—are painted yellow.

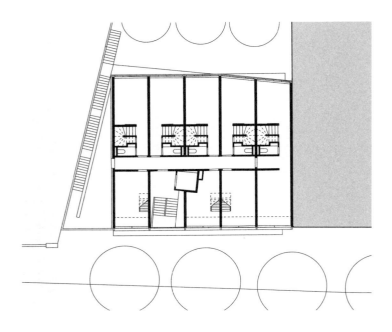

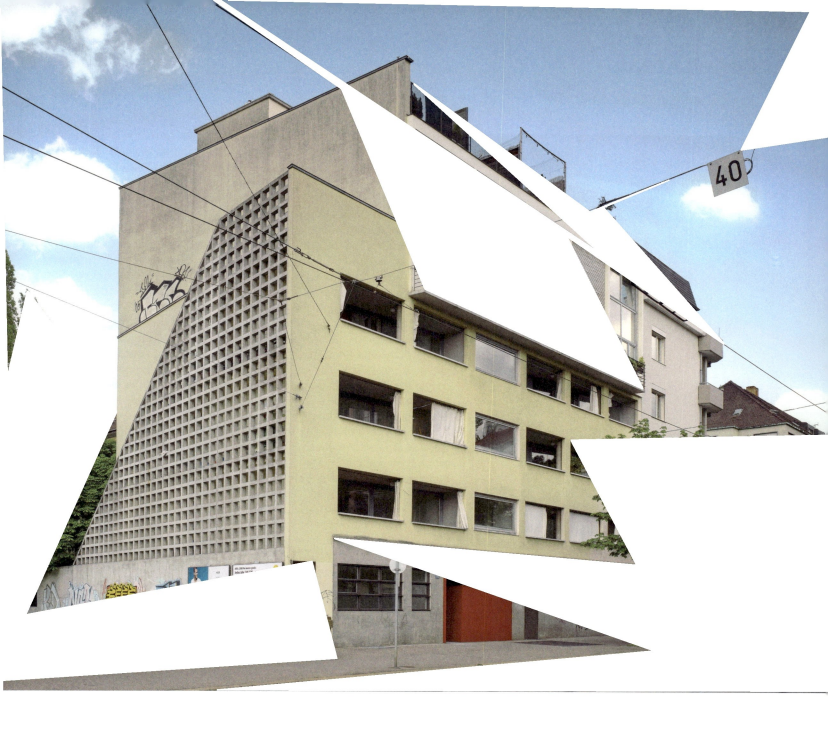

Bener Areal

Apartment Buildings, Chur, Switzerland, Competition, 1985

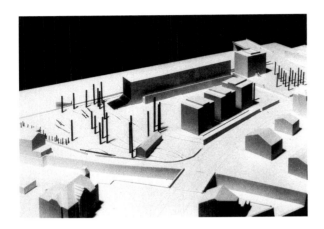

Formerly standing on the site near the old town were a villa and service buildings, along with orchards, which were contained by walls. To the west, the area is delimited by the sunken railway tracks. The villa was to be demolished.

The design by Diener & Diener uses fragments of the site to create a large courtyard, delimited on each side by apartment buildings, which preserves the memory of the earlier utilization. These too are contained by a wall, endowing the development with clear boundaries. Set above the railway tracks is an elongated apartment building which protects the courtyard from noise, while three urban villas stand on the opposite side. A neighboring parcel is occupied by an additional building.

The length of the apartment building is produced by coupling two units, with two apartments on each level. The bedrooms—all of them identical—are oriented toward the treed courtyard in the southeast, while living rooms and kitchens, as well as bathrooms and staircases, face the railway zone. Only the living rooms traverse both sides; their surface areas are nearly doubled by deep terraces that are set along the courtyard. The load-bearing structure, which is formed from supports, reinforces the typology of the apartments.

The urban villas form an ensemble that is composed of three closely situated volumes. Their typology is derived from traditional bourgeois apartment buildings in Grisons. The apartments—one per story—are subdivided by a central corridor that provides access to all rooms. Staircases and bathrooms are positioned at the center of the façade, so that the living room and equal-sized bedrooms occupy the corners and enjoy sunlight, which arrives from two directions.

The architectonic languages of these buildings differ dramatically, and correspond to their divergent typologies and construction methods: heavy, with masonry and equally sized windows for the three urban villas; lightweight, with supports and ribbon windows for the apartment building.

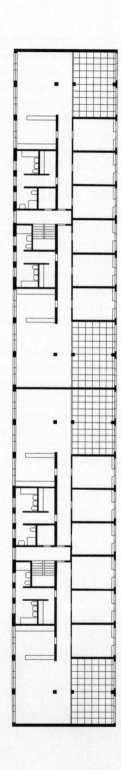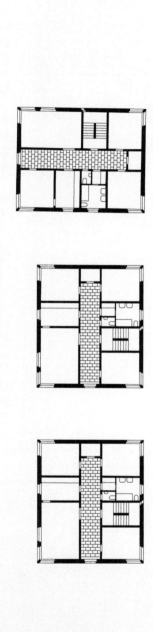

Hans Sachs Hof

Apartment Buildings, Salzburg-Lehen, Austria, 1986–1989

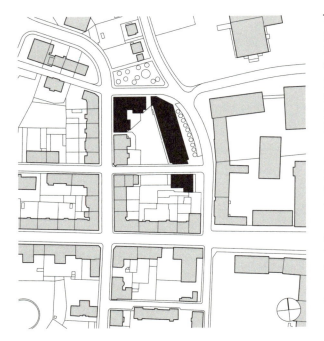

The district of Lehen represents a site of fracture within the city: here, perimeter block development yields to a newer, more open urban texture. In the project zone, perimeter block development exists only in fragmentary form. The Hans Sachs Hof consists of three clearly distinguishable parts. They are situated in a supplementary way alongside existing fragments, or else follow the building line of the new planning. In this way, this residential development illustrates the development of the city at this location in its successive phases.

The project area is subdivided by Hans Sachs Gasse. The fragmentary perimeter block development of the first section is carried further in the northwestern corner with new apartment buildings. Volumetrically, these follow the older buildings, while their load-bearing structure is different: each apartment is inscribed within a support grid as a *plan libre*.

The apartment buildings that form the northeastern part of the street block are set back from the street and stretch along a broad strip that is planted with trees. The load-bearing structure consists of parallel walls, which are angled somewhat toward the courtyard. The staircases provide access to three apartments per story. Two of these are deep and end-to-end; their bedrooms are oriented toward the street, and the living rooms toward the large courtyard.

The third building stands alone at the corner of Hans Sachs Gasse. Like the older apartment building opposite, it is tiered toward the courtyard, which is occupied by a number of single-story buildings and is closed to the street.

The apartment buildings accommodate shops in the ground floor. They differ from one another in the coloration of their plastered façades— orange, yellow, and gray-brown—as well as their windows. With the exception of the red buildings, the forms of the windows reveal the utilizations of the spaces behind them.

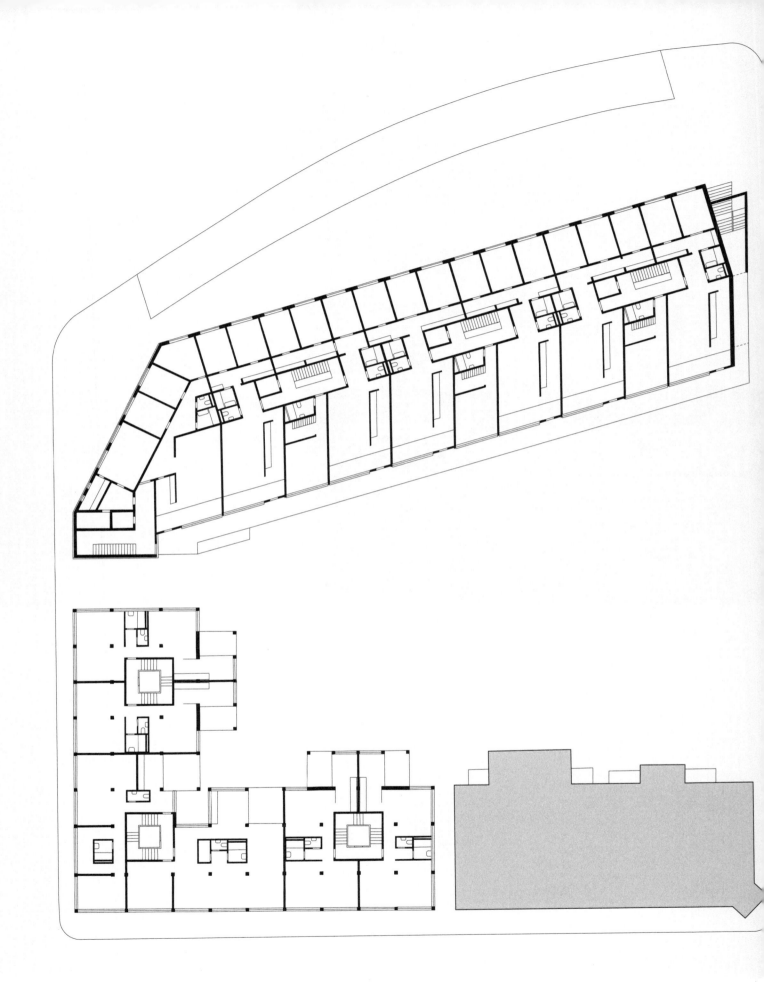

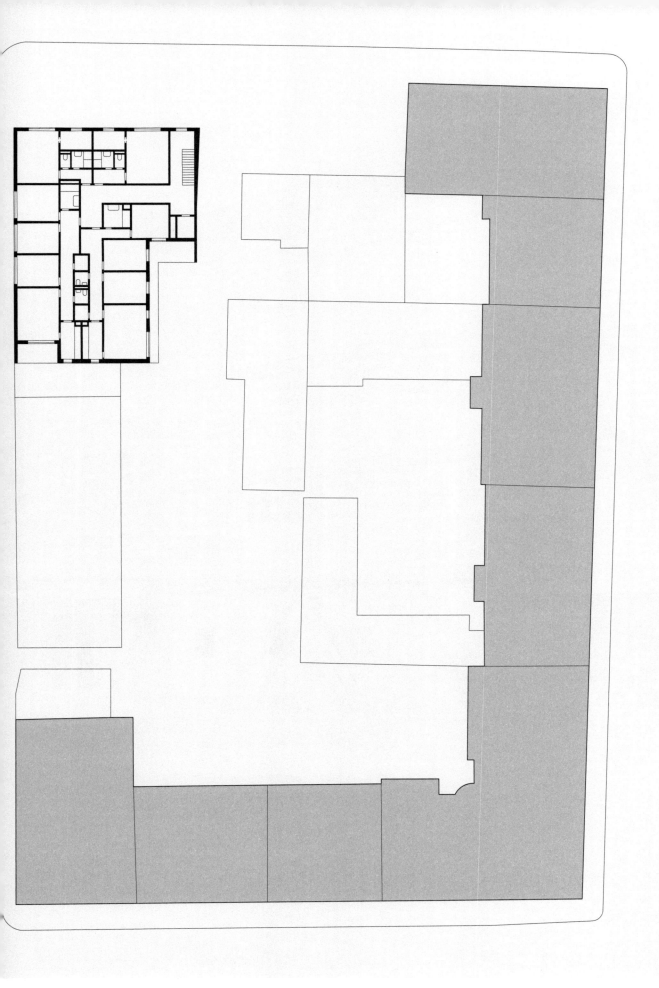

Luzernerring

Apartment Buildings, Basel, Switzerland, Competition, 1989

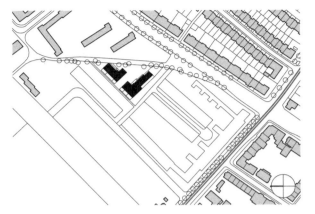

The parcel is situated at the western edge of Basel, between the city and the sparsely settled land along the French border. Following a site development plan, apartment buildings were developed through a competition for various parts of the extensive premises. The design by Diener & Diener is for a parcel on the interior of the area that is cut into a triangle by a pathway. The design subdivides the program into two apartment buildings whose characteristic attribute is the pronounced segmentation of the architectural volumes. Their angled configuration produces a courtyard that adjoins the park of a neighboring residential estate.

The buildings, which contain two and three apartments per floor, respectively, have divergent yet related forms. Their volumes are articulated sculpturally; they are tiered up towards one another. The floor plans, however, follow an identical principle: the staircase as well as the kitchen and bathrooms are grouped together on the courtyard side and form an elongated core, onto which the living and bedrooms are attached. These are oriented toward the south and west. The layer they create is uniform in configuration. This makes it possible to divide this layer into different rooms. Thanks to the configuration of the building, the living rooms are two- or even three-sided.

The façades are executed in plastered masonry. They are characterized architectonically primarily by the seemingly free play of windows, which are slightly larger for the living rooms then for the bedrooms. In the façades, this window figuration, which involves displacing them in relation to one another (a feature that has become common in contemporary architecture), generates an effect of fluctuation in the façades, while also allowing the rooms in the apartments to be partitioned freely.

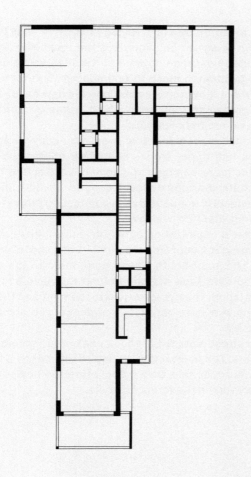
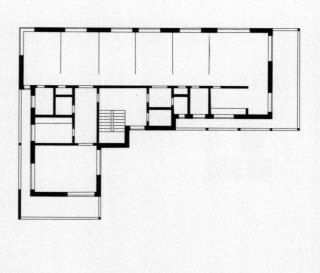

Rue de la Roquette

Apartment Buildings, Paris, France, 1992–1996

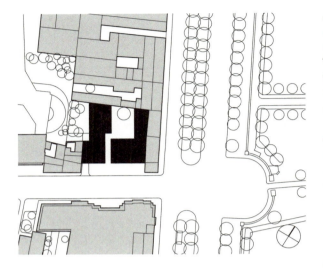

A *passage public*, recorded by a land registry map, that links the rear part of the parcel with the street, characterizes the urbanistic figure of this development, located near the entrance of the Père-Lachaise Cemetery. The buildings are positioned close to one another, and form a pair that faces the street, where they are set back along the new building line. Their interplay, as self-contained structures which define a traditional urban space, extends back into the courtyard.

Above a tall ground floor that is used for commercial purposes, the buildings have four upper stories and either one or two penthouse levels. Their peculiar forms emerged from their need to endow the development with a self-contained appearance. They differ in width and height, as confirmed on the Rue de la Roquette by the contrasting proportions of their uniformly positioned, identical windows.

The internal organization of the buildings mirrors their idiosyncratic forms, which extend deep into the parcel. Long and in places angled corridors lead to the apartments. These continue into the apartments themselves, whose rooms are set one behind the next, and are mainly one-sided in orientation. Their pragmatic arrangement and the urbanistic densification achieved here represent opposed yet complementary aspects of the design.

On the street side, the façades consist of limestone, and are plastered elsewhere. The courtyard is closed at the rear by a tall, old wall consisting of various materials. On a broad, plastered field, Dani Karavan has installed an artwork in the form of a poem.

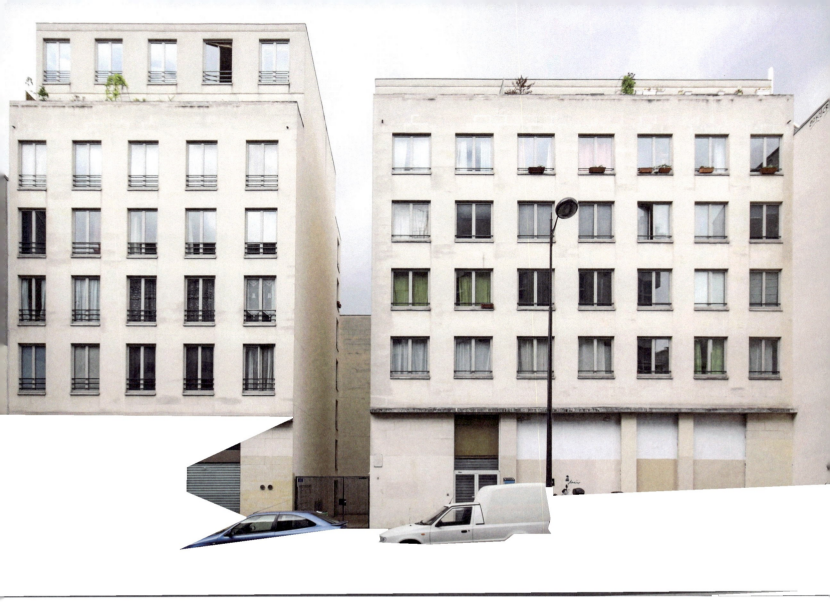

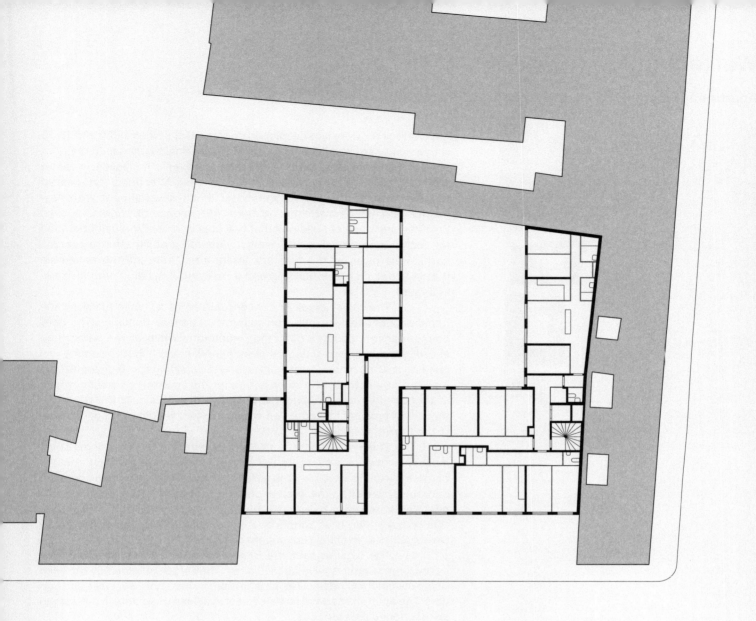

Warteckhof

Apartment Building, Basel, Switzerland, 1992–1996

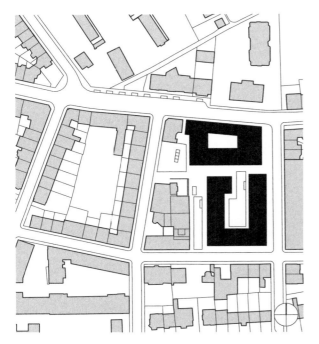

The Warteck Brewery was developed on this site between 1890 and 1935, with a number of buildings that constitute the final testimony to the presence of industrial architecture at the heart of Basel. The façade, in yellow and red brick, gives the complex formal coherence. After production ceased, the area was earmarked for perimeter block development with new residential and commercial utilizations. In response to protests against the disappearance of buildings that had characterized the neighborhood for such a long time, Diener & Diener prepared a design that preserves contiguous parts of the brewery, integrating them into an ensemble that includes an office building and a residential building with an open courtyard.

The street block is conceptualized as a public place, which remains permeable despite its occupation by these buildings. The composition accommodates planning regulations while at the same time allowing the buildings a degree of independence. While the commercial building on Grenzacherstrasse runs along the building line, it diverges from it on the other street. The same is true for the apartment building, which is set back from the building line on both sides. This calls the perimeter block development into question, to some extent yielding the building line to the brewery buildings.

The ground floor is a mezzanine. Here, the windows of the apartments have masonry parapets. Set above it are four stories. Apart from the corners, the units are organized as follows: the living room opens onto the bedrooms, as well as the kitchen and wet rooms, which are attached to it laterally; a separate hallway can be created by means of a cupboard. This Warteck Plan is as simple as it is compact; it has been modified by Diener & Diener in many subsequent designs.

The façades take the form of walls in dark clinker brick into which large windows have been incised. They are subdivided by the lines of the casement windows. The parapets are formed from low walls and iron bars. The apartments have no balconies; available to tenants in their stead are sectioned roof terraces.

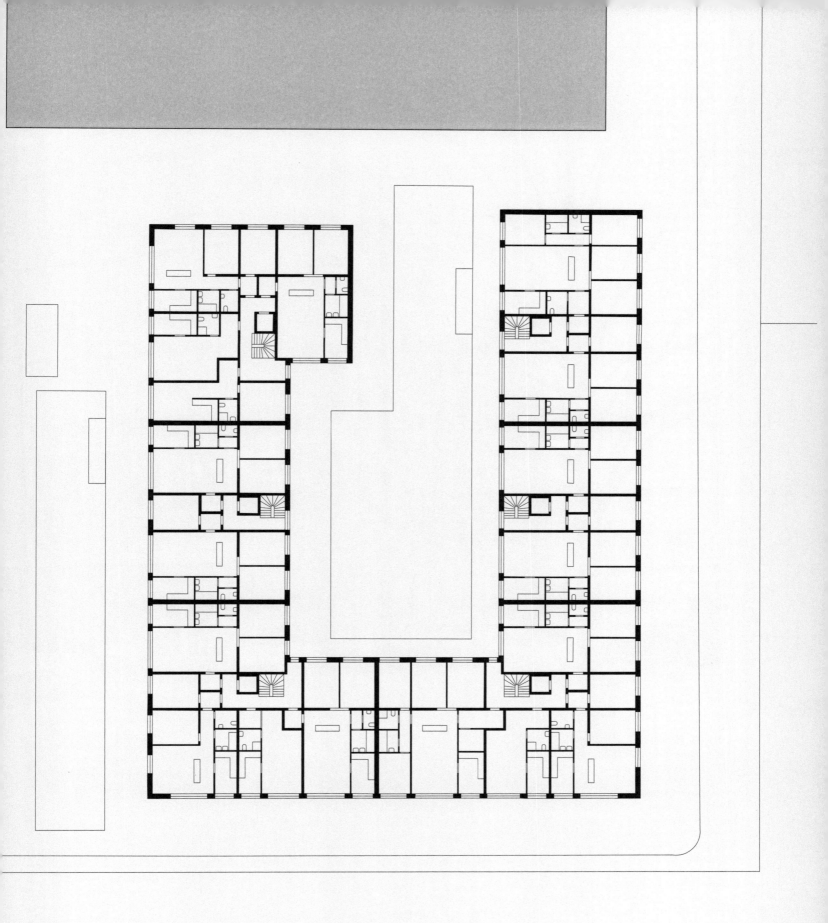

Hochbergerstrasse

Apartment Building, Basel, Switzerland, 1993–2002

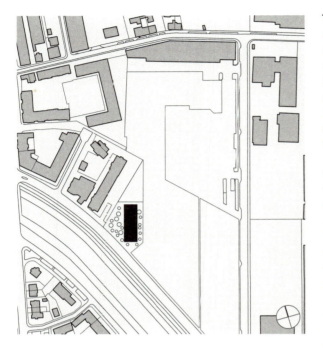

The eight-story apartment building stands at the edge of a residential zone on a site that was used until 1984 by the Basler Stückfärberei AG, and which served commercial and artistic purposes until 1997. Due to the configuration of the site, it stands at an oblique angle in relation to Hochbergerstrasse, a broad avenue, and the course of the Wiese River, and is adjacent to a large complex of shops and to the Hotel Stücki, built by Diener & Diener in 2001–2009. Originally, the investors planned to erect apartment buildings throughout the entire area, and in 1993, the architects elaborated a design consistent with this aim.

The building consists of three units, which are linked together to form a simple volume. The double-flight staircases are set along the façade, and each provides access to pairs of identical apartments on each floor. Typologically, they resemble the apartments of the Warteck Areal, except that they lack vestibules: one enters the living room directly. More important is another difference: set in front of the living room and the bedrooms are deep balconies that take up the entire breadth of the apartment. They provide the somewhat isolated, freestanding building with ambience, at the same time shaping its expression.

The architectonic language is both minimal and effective, and approaches a kind of architectural *degré zéro*. On the façades, its resources are restricted to the gray plastered parapets of the balconies and the walls between the apartments, which serve to subdivide the balconies. Nonetheless, the architecture is characterized by a lavish spaciousness. The ends of the building are plastered, and are windowless in conformity with the floor plan.

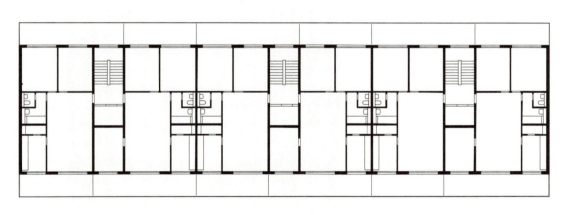

Parkkolonnaden

Apartment Buildings, Berlin, Germany, 1994–2000

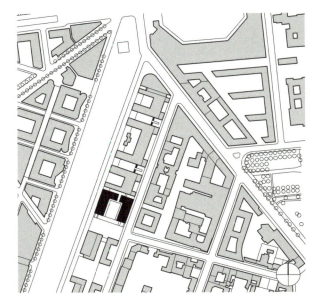

These two apartment buildings are inscribed into the framework of the master plan prepared by Giorgio Grassi. They form the southern end of a sequence of H-shaped buildings having diverse utilizations that runs from Potsdamer Platz toward the Landwehr Canal. The development as a whole is accompanied to the west by an elongated park that demarcates the track field of the former Potsdamer Bahnhof railway station.

Within the stipulated figure, the buildings form a pair of L-shaped volumes. Each has a ground floor and eight stories, with the building on the east being stepped on the eastern side, which faces the adjoining neighborhood. The buildings are separated by a narrow passageway which leads to a courtyard that is set above the S-Bahn (city railway), one story above street level. The courtyard, planted with pine trees, is open toward the south, where it is contained by a fluted concrete wall, which is gradually being overgrown in moss.

Set in the ground floor along the street are shops, while the upper stories accommodate seven and eight apartment units respectively, which form a kind of collage consisting of various types that recur in the projects of Diener & Diener. The one and two-story apartments are suitable for diverse lifestyles, while also making it possible to skillfully exploit the depth of the buildings and each apartment's specific location in its layout.

The façades, in red clinker brick, play with two contrasting figures. Toward the street and the courtyard, they display a uniform grid of posts and beams that is filled in by low walls and large, bipartite windows with glass parapets. In contrast, the façades on the front end of the buildings are treated as flat surfaces, and are articulated by a play of staggered windows whose positions appear random.

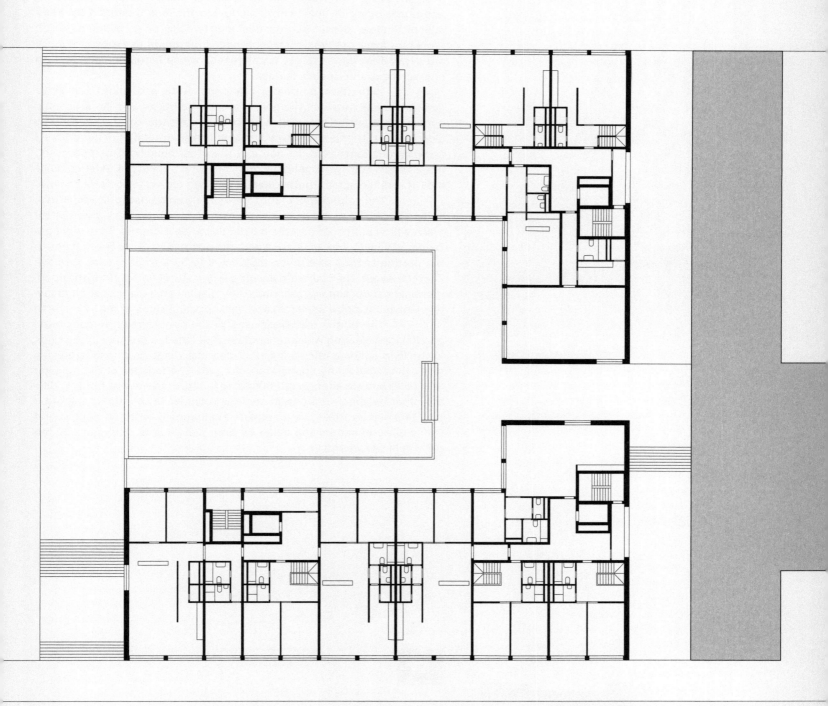

KNSM and Java-Island

Apartment Buildings, Amsterdam, Netherlands, 1995–2001

A new urban neighborhood has taken shape on a disused dock at the Port of Amsterdam. The master plan prepared by Jo Coenen envisioned an additional block of apartments alongside the one designed by Hans Kollhoff. Instead, Diener & Diener designed two apartment buildings which represent a marked typological contrast. With regard to expression, both are dependent upon the old warehouses, whose industrial architecture characterizes the locale's history.

With their emphatic presence, both apartment buildings generate a link between the genius loci of the docks and the urbanistic concepts actualized here. The first building is elongated, and lies directly along the water; it is a narrow volume whose sculptural form generates a complex relationship to the context. The other building is compact, and has a narrow courtyard; set back from the water behind pre-existing buildings, it is reminiscent—both formally and with regard to scale—of a hotel.

The ground floor of the long building contains studios for artists and artisans. The apartments in the seven upper stories have diverse floor plans which correspond to the building's variable depths. They highlight Diener & Diener's preoccupation with the adaptation of recurrent types to the particular form of a given building, and here in particular with the Warteck layout. The courtyard building is one story shorter. Here, the apartments are accessed via galleries. They display an exceptional typology: two individual rooms are accessed from opposite sides of the living room.

The tunnel formwork used in the construction necessitates parallel load-bearing walls in concrete. The façades are clad in red brick. In the long building, they consist of identical windows whose large size gives the façades the appearance of a grid. The façades of the building with courtyard are strongly differentiated in expressive terms: two are—like the other building—uniform in configuration, while the others feature a play of *pleins et vides* that contrasts emphatically with the neutral grid. The sculptural impression made by both buildings is reinforced by the glazing of the verandas.

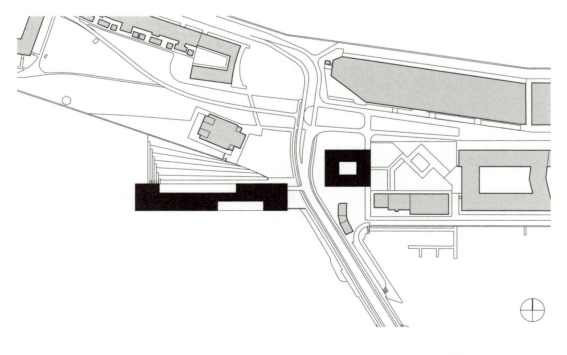

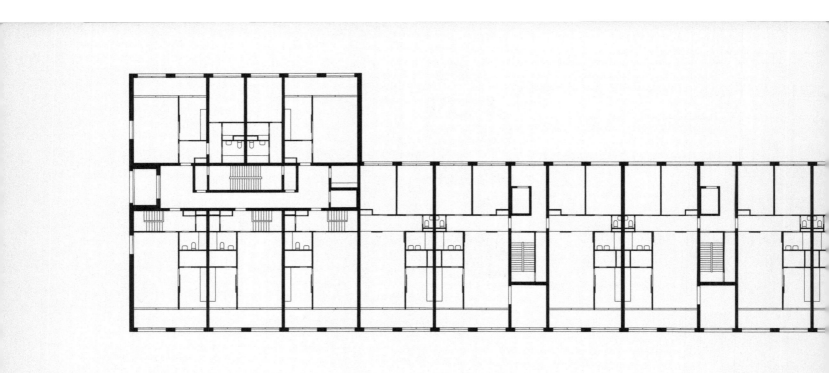

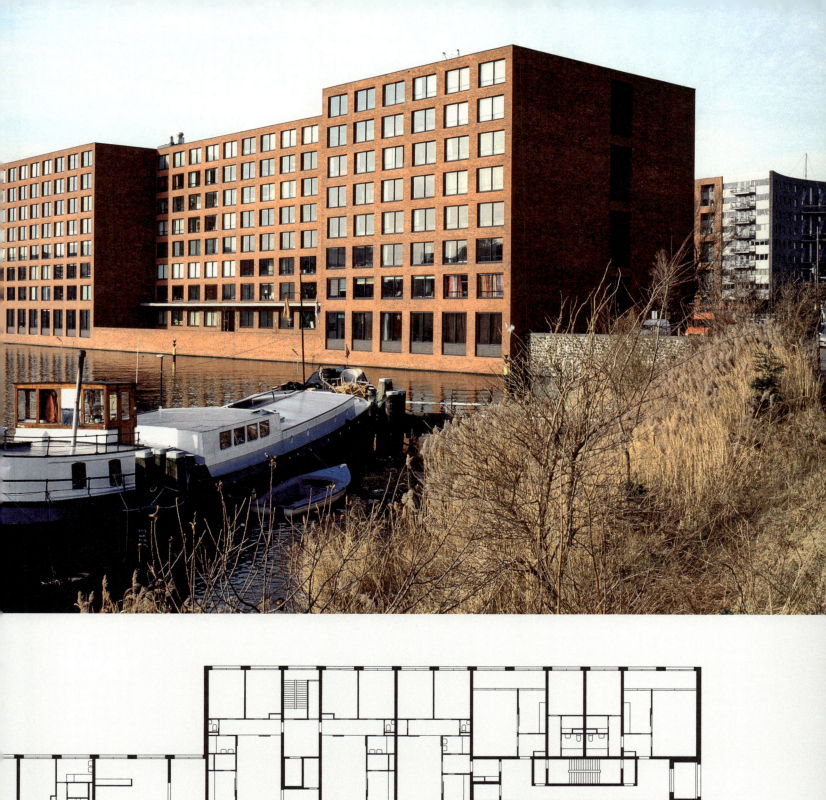
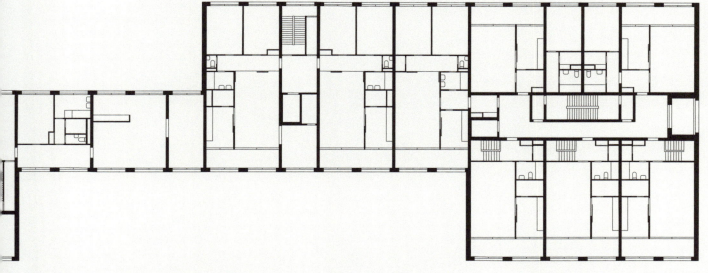

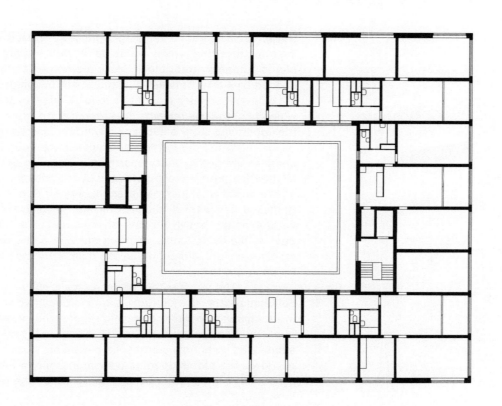

Schönaustrasse

Apartment Building, Basel, Switzerland, 1996–2002

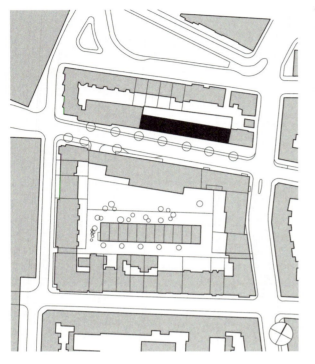

The Schönau apartment building supplants a remarkable commercial building from the 1960s, which occupied the entire depth of the parcel. It completes a narrow street block, leaving a correspondingly small courtyard, divided by a wall, between the apartment buildings. On Schönaustrasse, the sidewalk broadens out into a relaxed urban space, planted with trees, which nonetheless remains a *rue corridor*. To satisfy legal requirements, the uppermost story is set back toward the courtyard.

With a ground floor and four upper stories, the tripartite building contains altogether thirty apartments. Because Schönaustrasse slopes slightly, the parts are characterized by the minimal vertical displacement of the windows. Floor plans are identical: Schönaustrasse is heavily trafficked, hence the decision by the architects to configure the staircases, bathrooms, and eat-in kitchens on the street side. The eat-in kitchens are open to the living rooms, allowing the 2.5- and 3.5-room apartments to receive sunlight, although they are mainly oriented toward the courtyard, which lies to the north.

The arrangement of the rooms is visible on the façades. Along Schönaustrasse, the identical, slightly horizontal windows give the building a closed appearance. In this regard, the façade echoes the hotel opposite, also designed by Diener & Diener. In the courtyard, the façade is subdivided by narrow continuous balconies; with their identical vertical windows, the rooms open onto them at uniform intervals. The pedestal zone is clad in concrete panels, above which the façades are plastered in white.

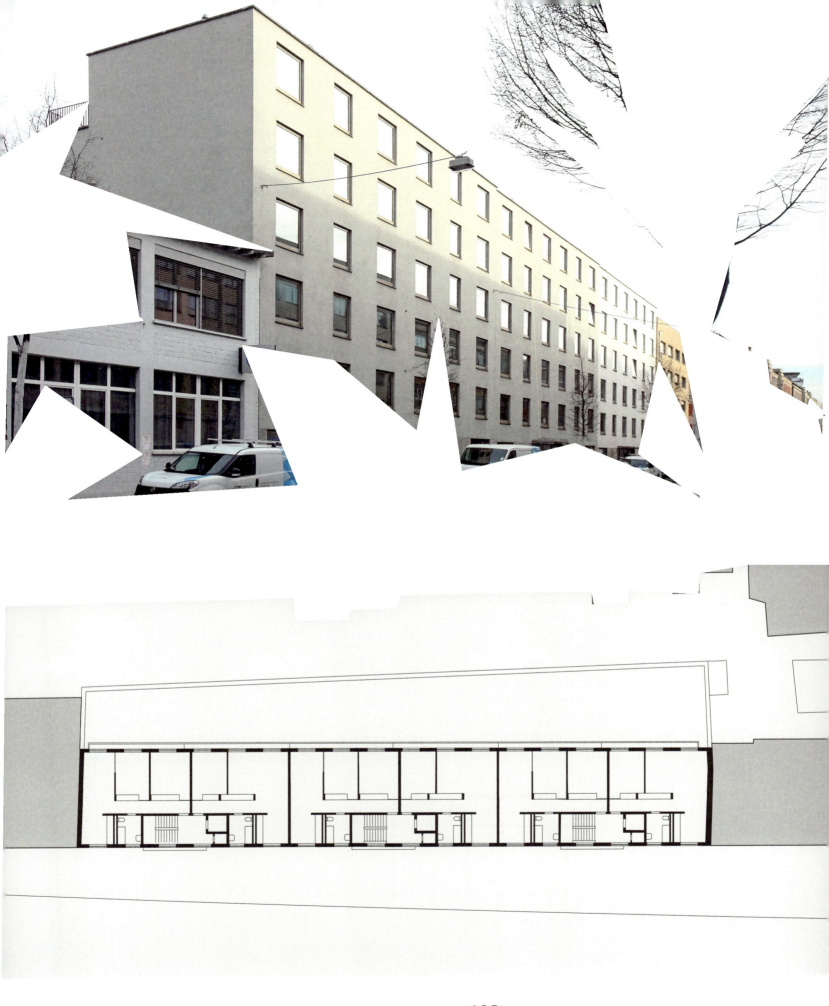

Elsässerstrasse

Apartment Building, Basel, Switzerland, 1996–1997

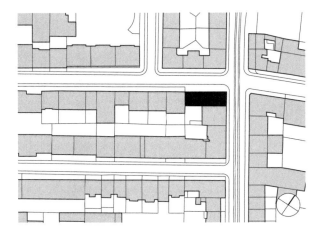

This small residential and commercial building is located on Elsässerstrasse in the St. Johann district, from which a tramway line extends to the French border near St. Louis. The neighborhood—originally populated mainly by blue- and white-collar workers—is characterized by four-story apartment buildings from the late nineteenth century. The plot forms the corner of a street block; accordingly, it has no courtyard, and is uncommonly narrow. The new building replaces two smaller, older apartment buildings, neither of which satisfied contemporary requirements, structurally or technically; they were ultimately demolished.

Currently, the ground floor is leased to a restaurant. The entrance to the apartments lies on Elsässerstrasse. Each of the four upper stories contains three apartments having either 2.5 or 3.5 rooms. The staircases, kitchens, bathrooms, and corridors form a layer of service rooms that runs along the long firewall on the side of the courtyard. The living and bedrooms are oriented unidirectionally toward one of the two streets. In conformity with building regulations, the fifth story forms a penthouse level.

The building is conspicuous by virtue of its color: the façades consist of red-stained concrete, and are articulated uniformly with horizontal, subdivided windows. The longer windows in the ground floor demarcate the pedestal zone and its commercial utilization. The building thereby employs straightforward resources in order to convey the urban character of this residential and commercial building.

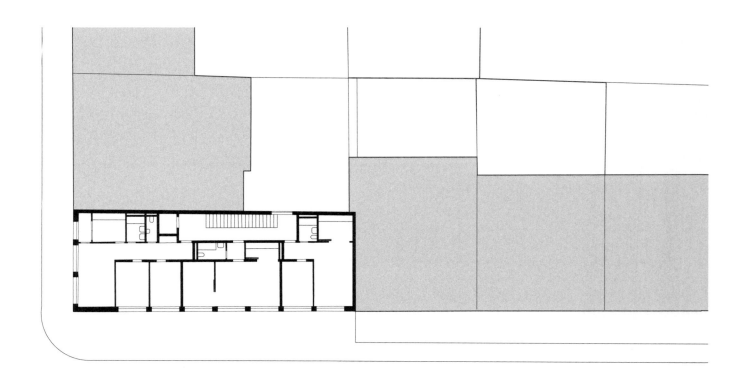

Ypenburg

Apartment Buildings, The Hague, Netherlands, 2000–2003

Ypenburg was formerly a military airfield located southeast of The Hague. After World War II, the site was used for civil aviation; in 1992, operations ceased and the site was earmarked for residential and commercial purposes. The extensive settlement consists of numerous neighborhoods. The residential buildings realized by Diener & Diener are located in Sector 6, for which three architectural practices prepared and subsequently realized designs in conformity with the site development plan created by West 8. Most of the buildings are two- or three-story row houses. In order to give the settlement a lively appearance, ensembles of buildings by a given architect alternate in random sequences. At certain locations, tower buildings set accents within a given sector.

The buildings designed by Diener & Diener are based on four different types. Story heights are oriented toward the intended uses of the rooms; in all instances, however, the uppermost story is considerably taller on the street side because of the slanting roofs. The façades, which consists of brick of varying darkness, are articulated by concrete cornices. Set between these at irregular intervals are the room-height windows. As a consequence of the varying heights of the buildings, the longer lines formed by the pale cornices are broken up.

In one part of the sector, the two- and three-story row houses are interfused with four "wild" buildings having up to sixteen stories each. Because they contrast with one another by virtue of their respective heights and the coloration of the brickwork, they are well-integrated into the larger order of the estate. Each access point serves two apartments; their individual identities are however expressed on the façades. Living and bedrooms are clearly separated by wet rooms; living rooms are extended by verandas. Toward the street and the gardens in the courtyard, ribbon windows emphasize the unity of the individual "houses." On the sides, external firewalls are broken up by narrow windows.

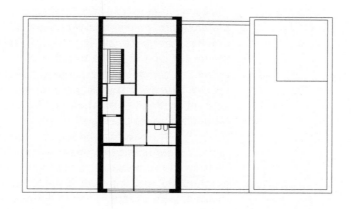

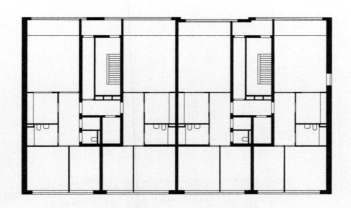

Renaissance

Hotel and Apartment Tower, Zurich, Switzerland, 2002–2011

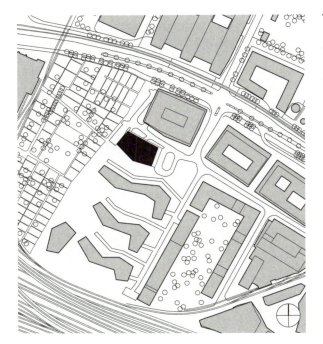

The tower stands on a large site west of the Maag machine factory. Used previously for commercial purposes, the site is part of a new urban district that has emerged in Zürich-West. The site development plan, prepared by Diener & Diener in 2000 together with E. & M. Boesch Architekten, prevailed in a competition, but was subsequently modified in a number of respects. The tower stands at the former location of a warehouse with offices built by Werner Stücheli in 1957 for the Coop firm, and which was originally to have been preserved.

The tower provides an ordering element for the surrounding, lower residential development by Meili Peter Architekten, delimiting it in relation to the adjacent park. The tower has twenty-four stories, and a height of 81 m. Contained in the lower stories is a hotel with 300 rooms together with a restaurant and conference and function rooms, while the upper nine stories contain apartments of various sizes with diverse floor plans. The entrance lies to the north on Maschinenstrasse. Elevators transport users to spacious halls from which the apartments are accessed. Each story takes the form of an irregular, five-sided surface. Service rooms are grouped around a bracing core with two emergency stairwells. Deviations from the right angle are restricted to the window fronts, and generate enthralling relationships between living areas and the surroundings.

The façades are clad in Roman travertine. They form a smooth volume that is subdivided vertically in ways that are dependent upon the utilization of the given story. They are wider in the apartments than in the hotel rooms, so that the façades appear more permeable above. This interplay of window sizes makes it more difficult to estimate the height of this otherwise homogenous tower. Apartment windows are room-height, and apart from minimal differences, identical: some have two casements and glass parapets, others are non-adjustable. They provide living spaces with a vertiginous view of the expansive railway facilities.

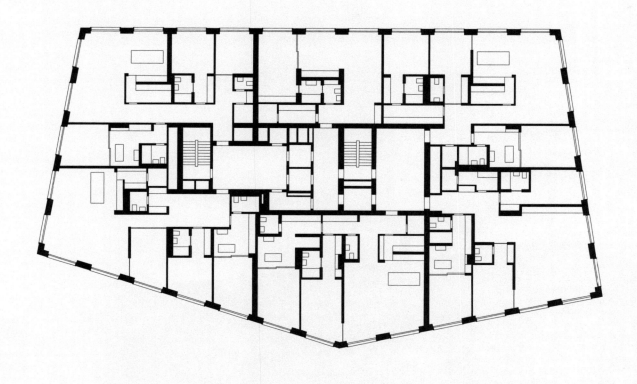

Maaghof West

Apartment Building, Zurich, Switzerland, 2002–2013

The Maag site encompasses properties by various firms; its name, however, comes from the Maag gearwheel factory. After the plant was relocated in 1991, a competition for a site development plan was organized; in the year 2000, Diener & Diener—in a collaboration with E. & M. Boesch Architekten—emerged victorious. Individual large volumes were to have been preserved and reutilized, with the addition of others contributing to the significant densification of the area. The core was planned as a landscaped courtyard that opens toward the railway tracks.

The elongated apartment building delimits the courtyard to the west in relation to the adjoining square-like surfaces of the new neighborhood. It is ten stories in height and consists of six connected parts. Two passageways lead to the courtyard. The ground floor is occupied by long, narrow residential studios and the upper stories, grouped around an internal hall, contain apartments featuring diverse typologies: positioned between two- and three-room apartments, with living rooms on the west and eat-in kitchens and bedrooms on the east, are unidirectional, two-room apartments. All apartments are extended toward the west via continuous balconies.

The façades are clad in vertically offset clinker brick in a range of sand tones. The building's appearance is shaped in particular by the balconies. These are carried below by angular—and beginning with the second story, rounded—supports which subdivide the western façade at uniform intervals. Positioned between the supports are parapets in gray concrete which imitate garden walls formed from round bricks, of the kind familiar from the nineteenth century. They form a permeable boundary between interior and exterior. In the first story, these project downward into the first story, merging these two stories to form a pedestal zone. On the eastern façade, the parapets in front of the windows, which extend downward to the floor, take up this ornament, unifying the building's architectonic language.

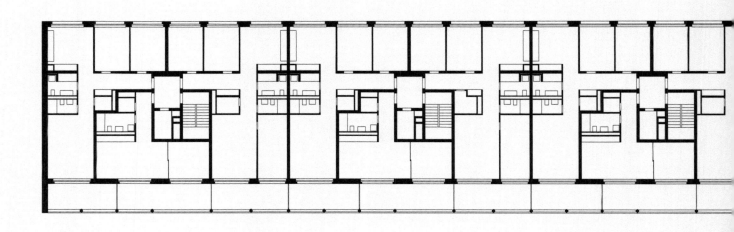
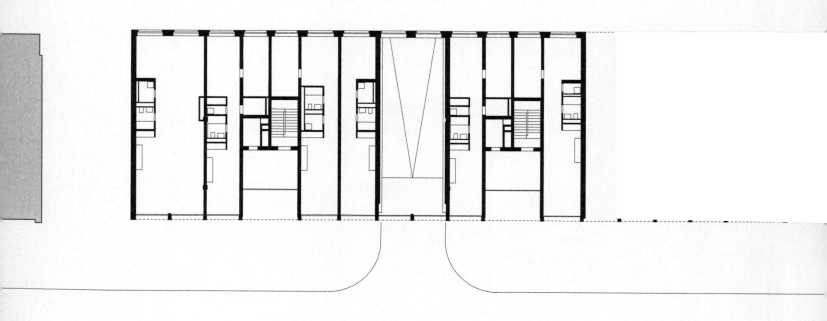

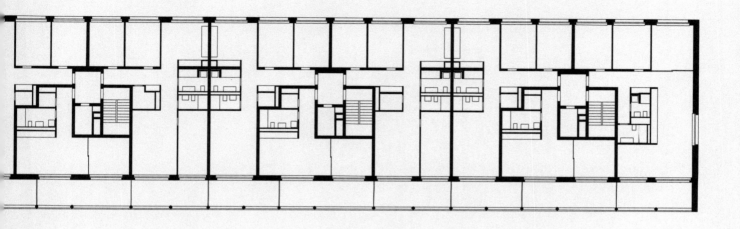

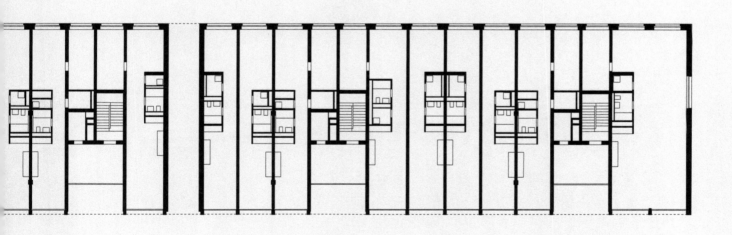

Casa A1, Olympic Village

Apartment Building, Turin, Italy, 2003–2006

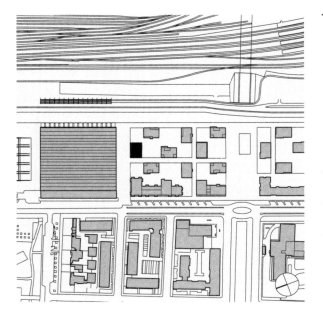

This residence for the accommodation of athletes during the 20th Olympic Winter Games, held in Turin in 2006, stands at the edge of the "chessboard" field stipulated by the master plan prepared by Steidle Architekten of Munich, and across from the converted halls of a central market for fruits and vegetables. It became an ordinary apartment building after the conclusion of the Winter Games. The intention was to preserve the special atmosphere of this building, a place where athletes from various countries were able to mingle freely.

The building dimensions and the grid of the load-bearing walls used by the designers were predetermined by the master plan, as were the locations of the entrances. Based on these requirements, Diener & Diener developed a typology that sidesteps a conventional subdivision of functions within the units. The rooms are interchangeable. Thanks to the uniform spatial structure of the apartments, users can decide freely where they want to eat, live, work, and sleep. There are multiple units on each level, each with an individualized arrangement of rooms and verandas. In the upper stories, there are also courtyards.

In order to heighten the sculptural impact of the vertical volume, the façades are plastered in two different shades of gray. The façade designs correspond to the apartments within, which vary from story to story. The play of windows of contrasting types and sizes, which are moreover staggered both horizontally and vertically, effectively annuls any sense of a simple segmentation of the stories. The result is an impression of precariousness that is underscored by the projection of the uppermost three stories, which face the converted halls opposite.

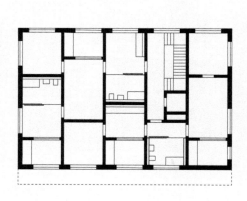
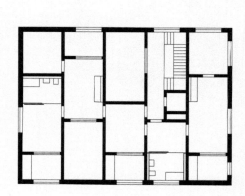

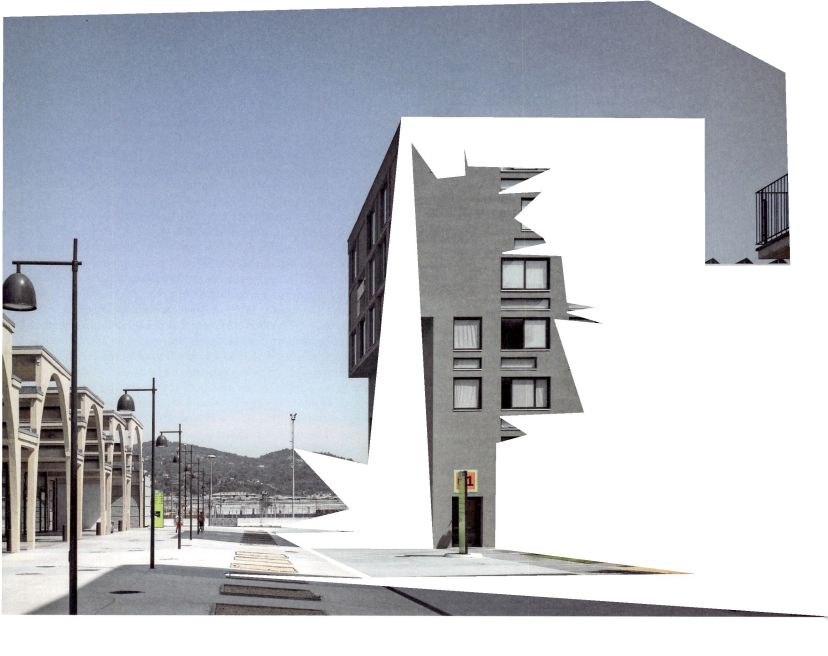

Westkaai

Apartment Towers, Antwerp, Belgium, 2005–2009

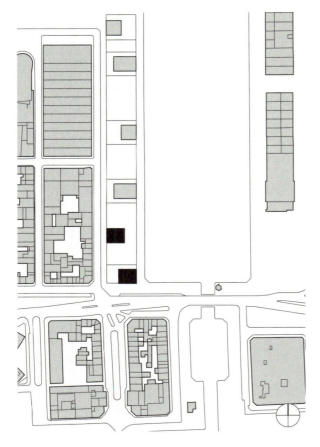

The Port of Antwerp, in the north of the city, was developed urbanistically after 2005. The undertaking was based on a site development plan, prepared by Diener & Diener, which envisioned six apartment towers. Each was to have approximately sixteen stories and to follow the edge of the harbor basin. Subsequently, they were erected in pairs by three different architectural practices.

The two apartment towers realized by Diener & Diener stand alongside one another, slightly displaced, at the start of the harbor basin near Amsterdamstraat. The surrounding neighborhood is characterized by old, narrow, stylistically diverse buildings. Emerging here is a dialogue with the locale: the vertical, graceful appearance of the towers, which preserves the permeable character of the expansive harbor area, makes an enthralling contrast with the dense patchwork of the existing development.

The apartment towers are 55 m tall and each accommodates circa forty apartment units in fifteen upper stories; the ground floors provide spaces for commercial activities. The stories are either 2.7 or 3.5 m in height, and the surface areas of the apartments range between 69 and 259 m². Thanks to an adaptable subdivision, rooms can be connected horizontally as well as vertically as needed. Configured around a core that contains wet rooms, the apartments are characterized by spacious living rooms. These extend along the façades and open onto verandas at the corners. Identical stories are repeated up to five times, with the larger apartments situated in the upper stories in particular, and smaller units in the lower ones.

The façades of the two towers are not identical, but resemble one another by virtue of their irregular network of windows and their cladding: the outer layer consists of fluted glass paneling which is mounted in front of panels consisting of aluminum and insulation. Depending upon the location, this materialization, employed repeatedly by Diener & Diener, ensures that the outward appearance of the two apartment towers varies continuously depending on light conditions.

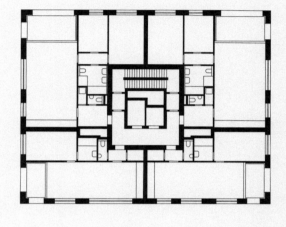
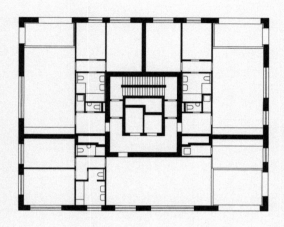
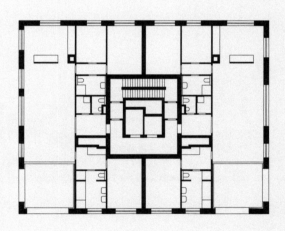
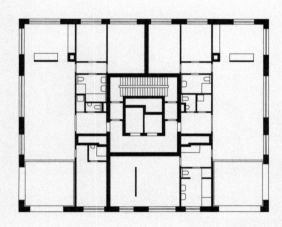

Île Seguin

Apartment Building with Day Care Center, Boulogne-Billancourt, France, 2005–2009

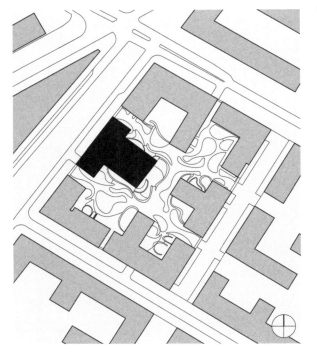

The large, T-shaped apartment building is a component of a street block in the former industrial site of the Île Seguin. Located at the western edge of Paris, the locale was once occupied by a Renault factory. Diener & Diener, together with Vogt Landschaftsarchitekten, won a competition for the site development plan. Individual parts of the project were subsequently awarded to various architects in France and abroad.

The urbanistic form can be read in two different ways: as a traditional perimeter block development with gaps between buildings, or as an agglomeration of apartment buildings having more complex forms. These vary in height, and enclose a multipartite urban locale whose atmosphere vacillates between garden and courtyard. The front walls of four of the apartment buildings define a center which is connected with the gardens. The courtyard is surfaced in gravel and given diverse plantings, reinforcing the character of an urban block perimeter development.

The apartment building by Diener & Diener encompasses two different programs: the ground floor and the first story are mainly occupied by a day care center; the seven and ten stories above respectively contain apartments with between two and five rooms. Access to all units is via two staircases positioned at the center of the building. The apartments are inscribed into the form of the building; some are two-sided in orientation, others are unidirectional. All open onto wide balconies.

The façades are distinguished by two contrasting forms of expression. Serving as parapets for the windows and balconies are prefabricated concrete elements whose design, the work of the artist Peter Suter, seem to absorb the flicker effect of the foliage of nearby trees. In front of the living rooms, these elements, provided with slits, form a layer that is detached from the façade and shapes the appearance of the building in particular toward the street. The other parts of the façades are smooth and closed; only in the courtyard does the front façade feature a small number of freely configured windows.

Île Seguin

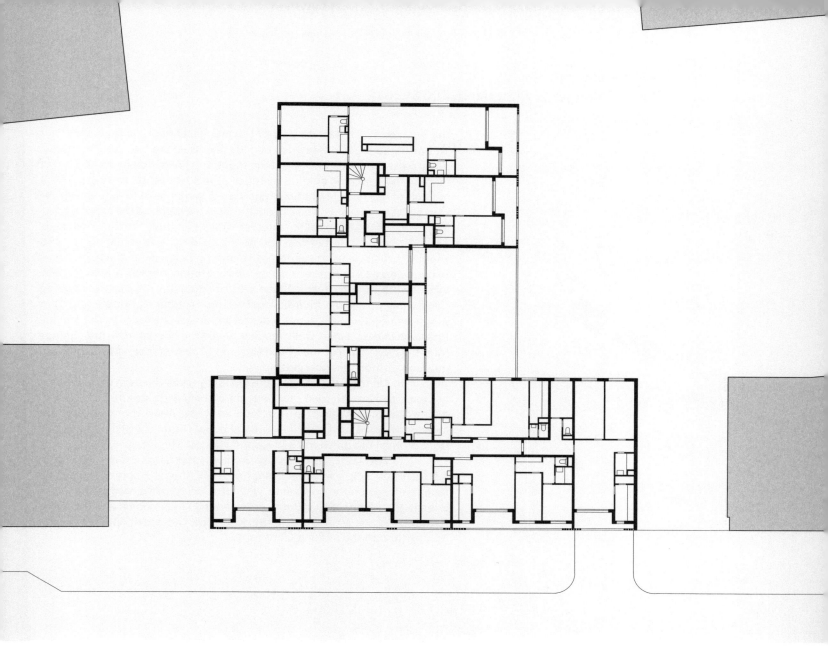

Schönwil

Apartment Buildings, Meggen, Switzerland, 2006–2012

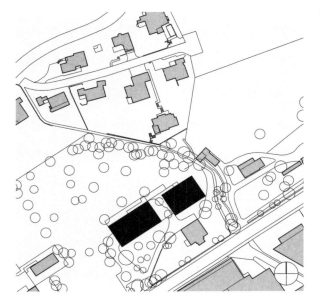

The site lies in the eastern part of the municipality of Meggen. Standing on Gotthardstrasse on terraces edged with stone are two villas surrounded by park-like gardens, and behind them, service buildings for the use in farming the adjoining fields. Embedded in this landscape setting will be a number of new apartment buildings, two of which have to date been realized by Diener & Diener. They lie on the same elevation as the service buildings behind Villa Schönbühl, together with which they form an ensemble.

Access to the two apartment buildings—which are displaced slightly in relation to one another—is via a pedestal zone that serves as a parking garage. For the sake of natural ventilation, the hall has large openings toward the courtyard; these are overlaid with the façade cladding, consisting of narrow boards mounted in an offset arrangement that produces regular gaps. In this way, the architecture alludes to the service buildings in the vicinity, while distinguishing the new apartment buildings from the classicism of the villa. The wood is painted pale gray in order to produce a chromatic relationship.

On the long façades, the cladding takes the form of bands that are expressed as pierced parapets in front of windows and balconies in a way that is familiar from rural buildings. Between the windows, the façades are clad smoothly in boards of equal width; the sliding panels in front of them are given the same appearance.

Each story contains two or three apartments having 2.5, 3.5, or 4.5 rooms each. In a way that is appropriate to the rural setting, bedrooms face the fields on the north side, while the living rooms face of the mountains in the south. Sliding doors between individual rooms and the living rooms generate a relationship between the two sides, inserting each apartment into the striking landscape.

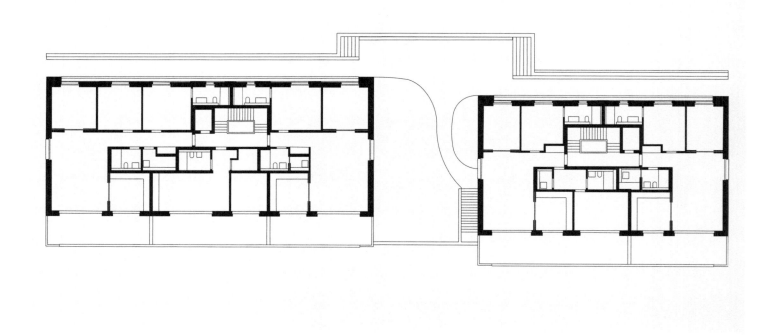

Markthalle

Apartment Tower, Basel, Switzerland, 2007–2012

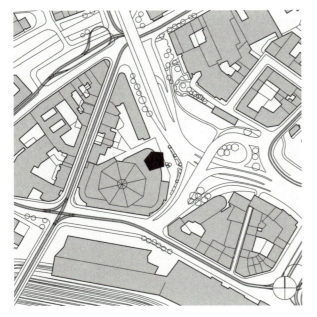

This Markthalle Tower stands directly between the octagonal Markthalle cupola from 1929—which has a span of 60 m and a height of 28 m—and the large office building constructed by Diener & Diener on Steinentorberg in 1988–1990. Its urbanistic form conforms to the plan that formed the basis for building codes tailored to the specific location.

The architects interpret the tower not as an isolated volume, but instead as a building whose layout is structurally similar to the Markthalle. The twelve upper stories above the level of the Markthalle form an irregular pentagon; each floor accommodates between two and four apartments. The rooms offer sprawling views of neighborhoods throughout the city. Bedrooms are oriented toward one side, and living rooms in the corners towards two sides.

The room-height windows of the apartments act like screens upon which a panorama unfurls itself from one end of the apartment to the other. For this reason, all rooms—including the bathrooms along the façades—are connected with one another by doors positioned along the windows. This generates spatial dimensions that are uncommon for such apartments; and in a neighborhood that suffers from significant noise pollution, this makes it possible to satisfy statutory requirements for the natural ventilation of interior spaces.

The segmentation of the façade is uniform throughout all stories, with windows in three different sizes, some subdivided, others not. Adjustable elements are secured by means of glass parapets. The façades have the appearance of an expansive grid. They are clad in panels consisting of reddish-brown aluminum, and on top of these, panels of rough glass. As a consequence of this façade assembly, the color of the Markthalle Tower alters dramatically depending upon changing weather conditions, ranging from pale green to dark brown. Hence its highly variable presence within the city; on some days, it almost seems to dissolve into air.

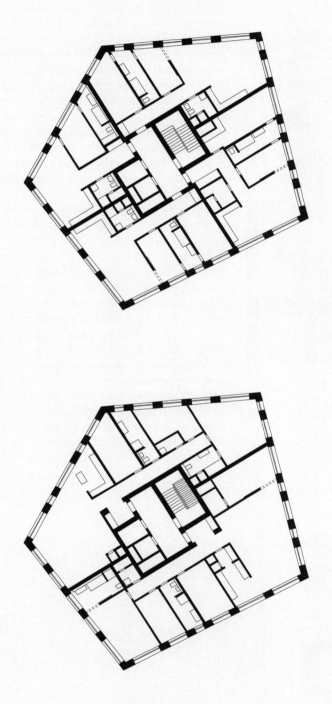

Favrehof

Apartment Building, Wallisellen, Switzerland, 2008–2014

The Richti area, situated south of the Wallisellen railway station, was used previously by a number of firms, in particular for the manufacture of cement products. After 1989, various projects developed the disused terrain for apartment buildings, as well as for commercial activities and service provision. In 2007, Vittorio Magnago Lampugnani prepared a site development plan for subsequent development; it was approved in 2009. The site, located at the periphery of Zurich, was transformed into an urban neighborhood with residential blocks, each designed by a different architectural practice. The neighborhood is characterized by diverse urban spaces such as squares, avenues, arcades, streets, and courtyards, all of them integrated into a network of green spaces.

Like the other blocks, the Favrehof, designed by Diener & Diener, has five stories and a recessed penthouse level. In conformity with the site development plan, the ground floor arcade accommodates shops, with apartments on the remaining three sides. Above the shops, a frieze executed in dry masonry work—the work of the artist Josef Felix Müller—accents the urban front of the building. The upper stories contain large apartments having 2.5 or 3.5 rooms. Living rooms traverse the building from front to back, making it possible to use the same typology on all sides of the courtyard. The balconies take up the entire breadth of the apartments: on three sides, they are oriented toward the courtyard; on the fourth side, toward the arcade to the south.

The architectonic language consists of wide pilasters which subdivide the façades. Positioned in the fields between them are the windows, which have varying widths depending upon the dimensions of the bedrooms; hence the differing intervals between pilasters. In front of the living rooms, these are detached from the façades and demarcate a balcony layer. Spanned between them are concrete parapets with pierced fluting which, with their flickering optical effect, produce a striking contrast with the massive pillars. All parts of the façade are insulated and plastered in white.

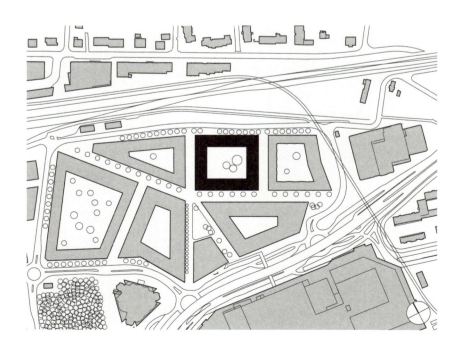

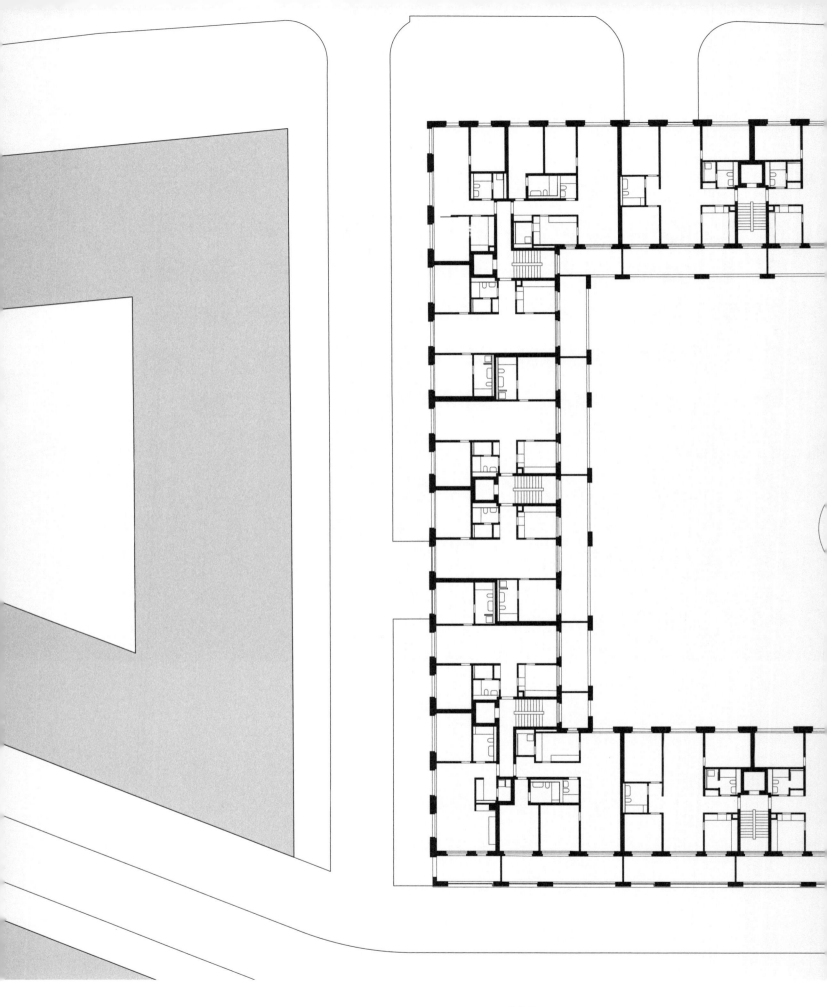

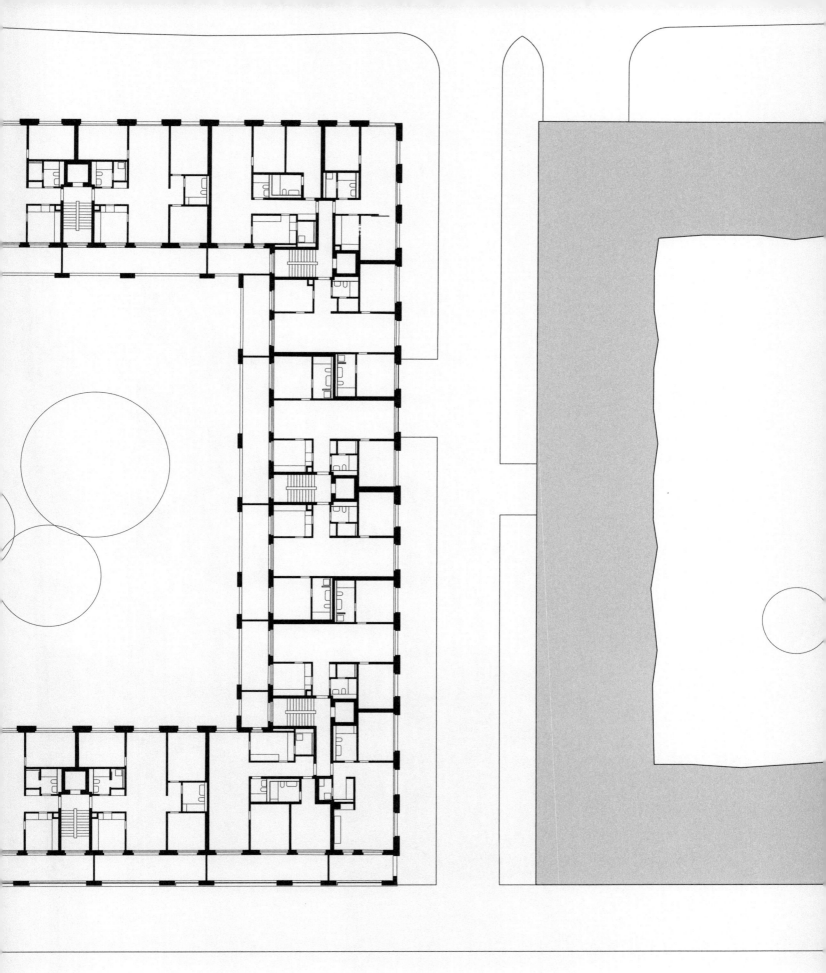

Via Suot Chesas

Apartment Buildings, Champfèr, Switzerland, 2008–2015

The pair of apartment buildings stands at the edge of the village, and of the building zone. Legal requirements permitted the construction of a building measuring 25 m in length. An initial project proposal corresponded to these criteria, but received objections from various parties. For this reason, but also because the apartments would benefit more from their extraordinary location at the edge of the plain if they were divided into two different structures, Diener & Diener developed a new project.

The apartments are owner-occupied, though four of them must be leased to local residents at rents that are customary for the region. For the most part, the three- and four-story apartment buildings are subdivided similarly. As a rule, there are two 4.5-room apartments per story. Living rooms are oriented toward the southeast, and look onto the open Grevas plain, which is used for agriculture, and extends all the way to the buildings. Concrete cores contain staircases and wet rooms. Like the inner and outer shells, the load-bearing structure consists of wood. The outer walls were prefabricated in the workshop and assembled on site. The ornamentation, reminiscent of the traces of bark beetles, was cut into the boards and battens of the outer shell. They are the work of the artist Josef Felix Müller. The boards are given a white glazed finish.

Toward the plain, loggias are positioned in front of the apartments; these are carried by rounded steel supports. The arrangement of the windows—which are set deeply into the façades—is irregular. They display diversely beveled reveals. In places, an additional narrow, laterally displaced window is set beneath the main window. As a result, the openings form an "all-over" pattern that serves to strengthen the sculptural character of both buildings.

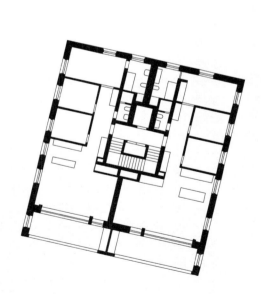

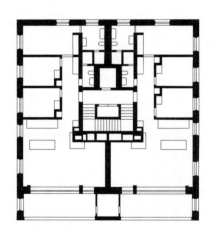

GreenCity

Apartment Buildings, Zurich, Switzerland, 2012–2018

The two buildings are elements of the master plan developed by Diener & Diener in 2014 for the site of the Sihl paper factory in Manegg. Situated between the slope of Entlisberg and the railway line, it comprises buildings for residential, commercial, and public facilities, as well as a large hotel. Only the spinning mill, built in 1857, testifies to its former utilization. Together with Spinnereiplatz in front, it forms the center of the new urban district known as GreenCity.

The architects built two apartment buildings in the northern part of the area. The larger one is U-shaped, like the other apartment buildings at the foot of the slope toward the east. At the rear, open courtyards lead toward the forest beneath the autobahn; in front, the buildings stand on an elongated plaza. Ground floor shops provide the buildings with an urban accent.

The smaller building by Diener & Diener is set back somewhat from this plaza, which yields space for a fenced urban garden. The five upper stories are given a back-to-back typology that is unusual for these architects: the two- and three-room apartments lie along either side of the wall that subdivides the building in a lengthwise direction. They face either east, toward the urban garden, or west. Living rooms traverse the entire depth of the apartment, with kitchens and bathrooms lying along the subdividing wall.

The two sides of the building are distinguished primarily through their façades. The balcony slabs are continuous. Toward the east, the living rooms—with their large windows—are oriented toward the urban garden. The glazed concrete frames stand on these slabs, like the windows of winter gardens. On the west, balconies run continuously in front of the apartments. Here, the glazed concrete frames serve as weather protection in front of the recessed living rooms, and reduce the noise from the railway line along which the building lies. The lateral façades are flat; the staggered configuration of small windows makes it difficult to relate them to the apartments inside, hence emphasizing the planar expression of these sides.

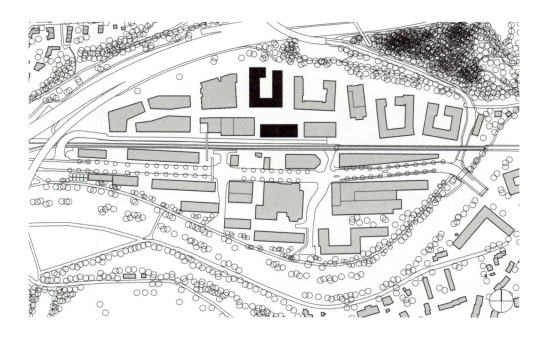

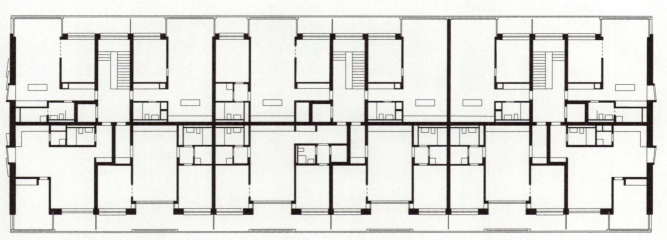

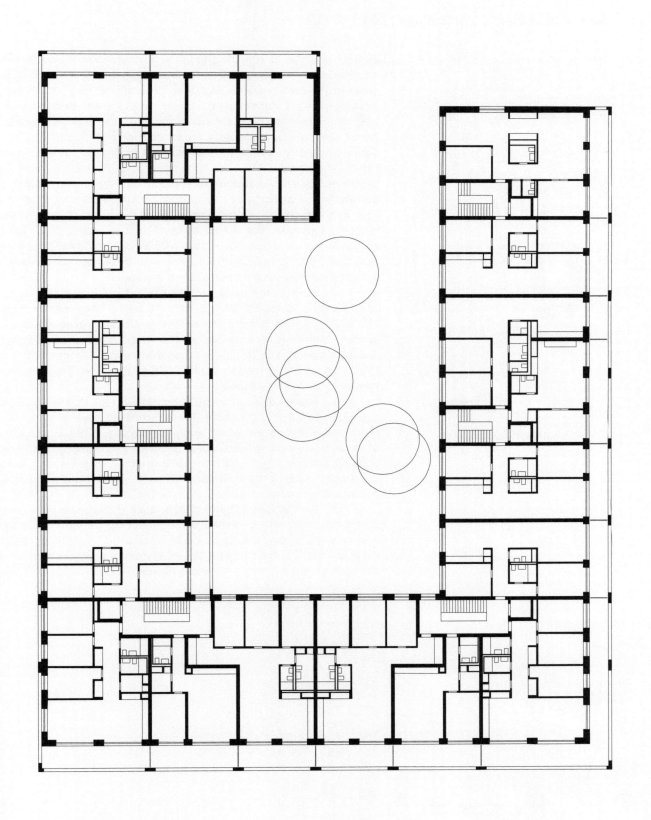

Hardhof

Apartment Buildings, Bülach, Switzerland, 2013–2019

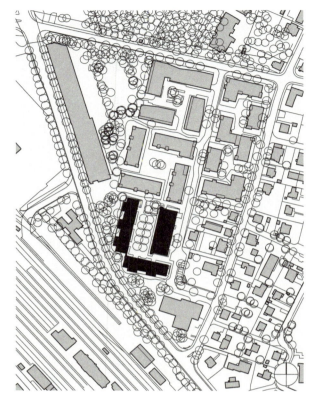

Beginning in the 1910s, the site in the northern part of Bülach was used as a foundry by the Sulzer firm. To distinguish it from other locations, the name of the facility was Bülachguss. Around the year 2000, operations were suspended. Subsequently, the municipality decided to develop the site—along with the adjacent site of the Glashütte Bülach, a former glassworks factory—into the new urban district of Bülach-Nord. In 2013, Diener & Diener was awarded the contract for the site development plan. The plan adopts the urbanistic form of the open courtyard, and is to be implemented by various architectural practices. Enjoying landmarks protection and testifying to the site's industrial past is the foundry building, which now accommodates a co-op and public functions. Diener & Diener is responsible for planning the zone known as the Hardhof, which lies on the corner of the site above the Bülach railway station. Toward the west, it is delimited by Schaffhauserstrasse, and on the east by Gussstrasse, which links the various construction sites in the area.

    Toward the heavily trafficked Schaffhauserstrasse, two multipart apartment buildings combine to form an angle. They feature a typology that is untypical for Diener & Diener: the vestibule is set against the façade, so that apartments are accessed via the living room. Bedrooms are oriented toward the courtyard. This means that only the living rooms face the street. The balconies are projecting, another untypical feature. They are displaced laterally to avoid shadowing the living rooms.

    The third, tripartite building has six stories, and closes off the courtyard toward Gussstrasse. The apartments have deep, continuous balconies with curtains, which are rounded at the ends. Through the play of curtains, they are reminiscent of an apartment building on the sea. The columns which carry the balconies are strikingly massive, and delimit the apartments toward the courtyard. Parapets consist of thin, twisted iron bands that generate an optical shimmering effect.

    The façades, in beige clinker brick, make an impression of monumentality: they are subdivided throughout their entire heights by broad pilasters, and endow the façades with a sculptural feel. Situated between them are vertical windows which underscore the impact of the façades, themselves reminiscent of Baroque palaces.

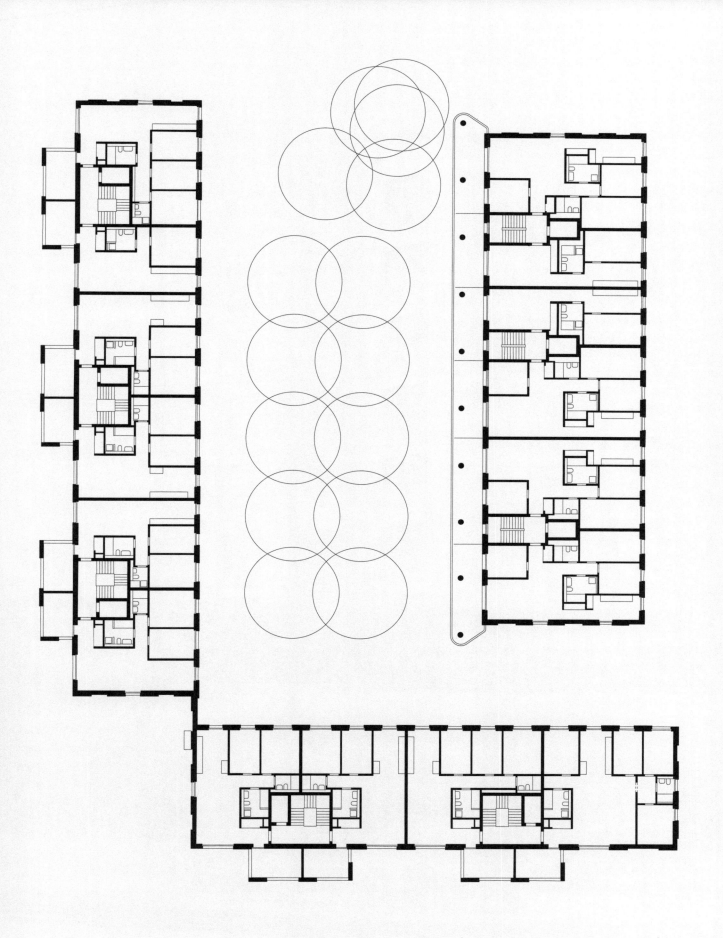

Prannerstrasse

Apartment Building, Munich, Germany, 2014 (unrealized)

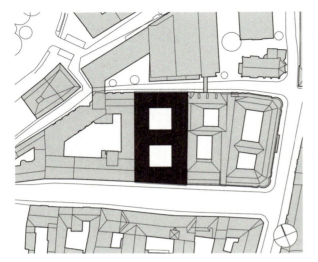

Urbanistically, this design for an apartment building in the Kreuzviertel neighborhood at the center of Munich takes up the traditional form of the townhouse that forms part of a closed building line, with its impressive façades, pitched metal-clad roofs, and precisely configured courtyards.

Accommodated in the tall ground floor are shops, along with the delivery facilities for the neighboring hotel, located in a landmark-protected building on Salvatorstrasse. Passageways lead into the courtyards from both streets, and into a common glazed hall with spacious staircases. The five-story building retains the organization of an upper-class residential building. In the apartments, this basic structure is however overlaid by a more contemporary conception. The distinction between rooms with structural and nonstructural walls is eliminated in favor of a load-bearing structure consisting of supports, into which the one-, two-, and four-room apartments are inscribed. In the interior, the traditional separation of the rooms is softened. Walls are set back from the façade, creating an enfilade; occupants move through the apartment along the windows. On the courtyard side, the penthouse level is set back 1.5 m from the façade, creating terraces for those apartments.

The façades differ depending upon location. On the street side, they consist of deep cast-stone frames that are positioned in front of the concrete, load-bearing structure. Set in front of the full-height windows are latticework parapets. In the courtyards, the support structure is clad and plastered. The façades, with their sculptural design, not only allude to the neo-Baroque palace, but also form thresholds between interior and exterior in the courtyards, ensuring residents with a degree of intimacy despite the minimal distances involved.

In the course of planning, the investors abandoned the design due to the minimal demand for small apartments at this location. Nor was a successor design for a building with larger and correspondingly more expensive apartments ultimately realized. For strategic reasons, the final result was an office rather than an apartment building.

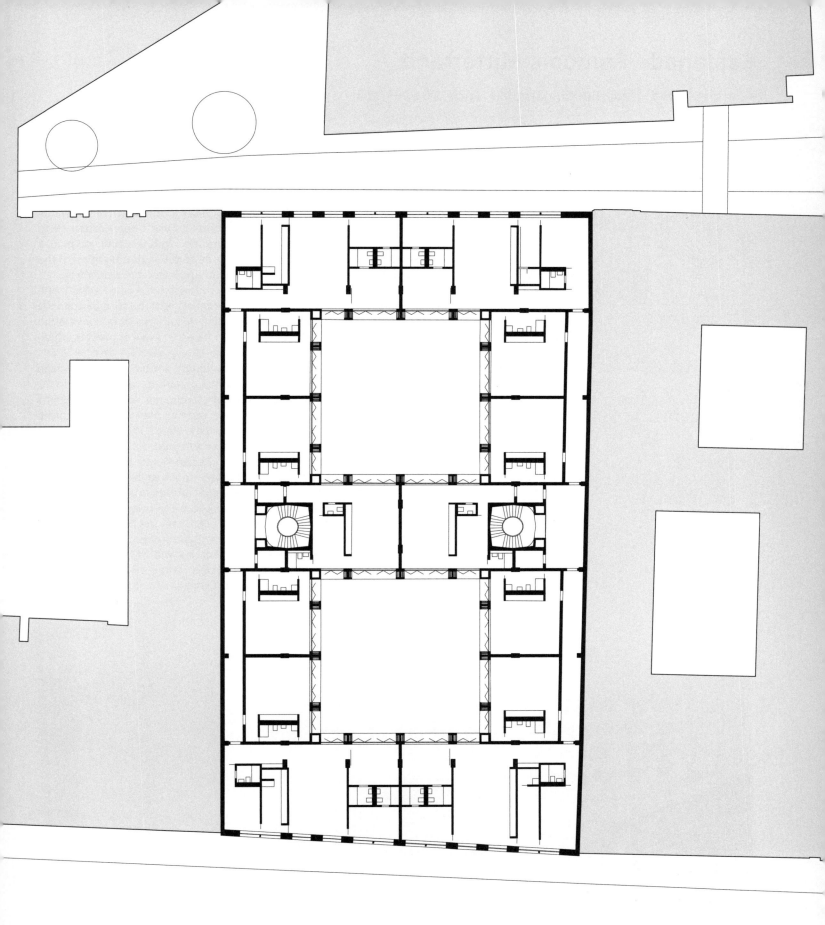

Esplanade François Mitterrand

Apartment and Office Building, Lyon, France, 2016–2020

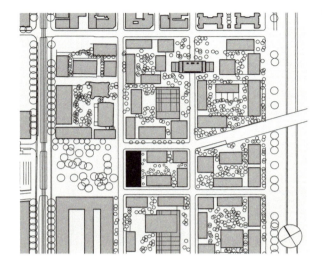

This residential and commercial building, designed by Diener & Diener in collaboration with Clément Vergély architectes, Lyon, and Joud Vergély Beaudoin architectes, Lausanne, stands in the La Confluence district, located at the meeting point of the Saône and Rhone Rivers. On the basis of a master plan prepared by Herzog & de Meuron, the district, once characterized among others by central markets, has experienced a fundamental transformation, though some of the old halls have been preserved to accommodate public utilizations. In accordance with the land use plan, a number of freestanding buildings contribute to the materialization of the traditional street block, so characteristic of Lyon, albeit in a new way.

The apartment building stands across from a new harbor basin on the Saône and a park, the Esplanade François Mitterrand, a particularly prominent location. Its status is confirmed by its superior height in relation to the other buildings of the block, and by its expressive character, which could be called monumental.

On the long sides of the building, double-story, concrete columns carry continuous balconies, which constitute a usable zone between the street and the apartments. The prefabricated, sculptural columns are rotated into various positions. The optical play of the resultant contrasting shapes generates a kind of dancing affect. The façades behind, in conventional plastered masonry, are subdivided by French windows, which are placed before both offices and apartments. Set between the columns are parapets consisting of twisted steel bands.

Providing access to the individual stories is a pair of spacious staircases, which are reminiscent of bourgeois apartment buildings. The ground floor is used by a restaurant. The offices on the first story and the apartments on the second to the eighth story, are freely configured on the floor slabs, which are supported by the façades and by the supports and walls at the center. Wiring and piping, and hence service rooms, are arranged around these supports, making it possible to convert apartments into offices and vice versa.

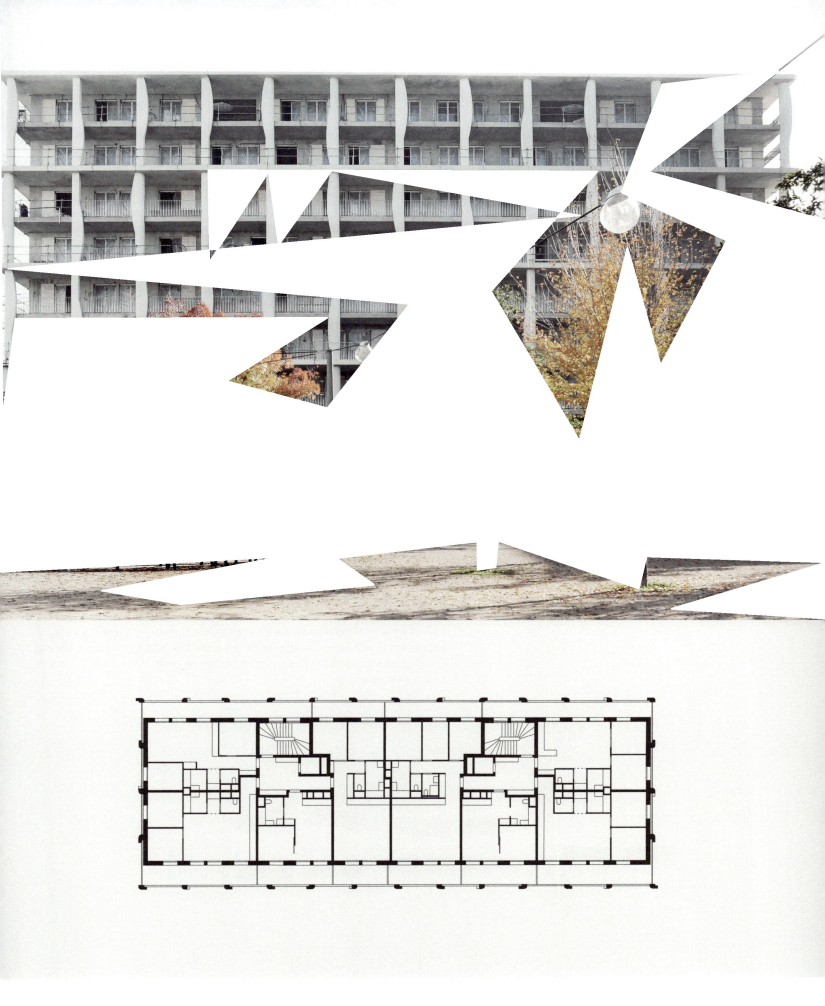

Weidmatt

Apartment Buildings, Lausen and Liestal, Switzerland, 2014–2020

This extremely large site extends along the base of a wooded slope that is cut through by a small valley. The lesser portion belongs to Liestal, the other one to Lausen. On the other side of the Ergolz River, the two communities have already grown together structurally. Until the 1990s, the site was used by the Cheddite firm to manufacture explosives. Two buildings have been preserved as witnesses to this industrial past. They are used commercially, and endow the locale with its specific character, one that goes beyond landscape features.

The site development plan was prepared by Diener & Diener in conjunction with Vogt Landschaftsarchitekten. The configuration of the buildings on the elongated area, with its southern orientation, conforms firstly to the former alignment of the demolished factories, and secondly to the characteristics of the site. The result is a lively arrangement of apartment buildings that lies along the forest and the river. The ensemble is subdivided into three clusters with spacious courtyards, given divergent shapes, which are planted with fruit trees.

The buildings differ in height. The rear buildings of the central clusters on the street have six stories each. This effects a concentration of the garden-style space that traverses the development. The buildings also display contrasting typologies. They explore the various spatial possibilities of dwelling in a way that recalls the housing estate exhibitions of the 1920s. Common to all is the potential inherent in rooms that extend through the entire apartment.

Both the load-bearing structures and the cladding of these buildings are in wood. The supports subdivide the façades at uniform intervals; the stories are inserted between them. They are distinguishable by virtue of the projecting boards which protect the cladding. In front of the full-height windows, the battens—which serve to cover the joints—form parapets. The same parapets are found on the balconies as well. The wood is impregnated with three different tones, an additional means of differentiating the volumes.

Currently under construction in Lausen are six buildings. Before four additional buildings can be erected on the territory of Liestal, an expert assessment will need to determine whether the administration building, which dates from 1916, is worthy of landmark protection as a document of the Heimatstil.

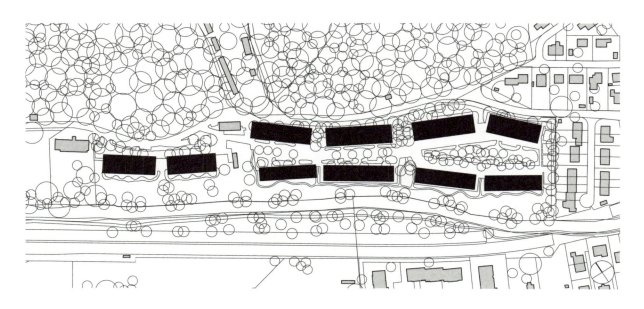

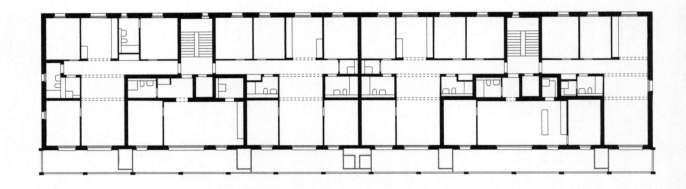
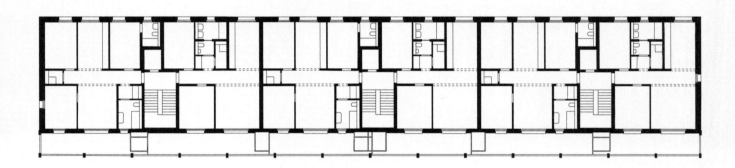

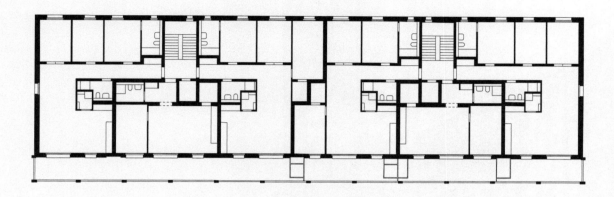
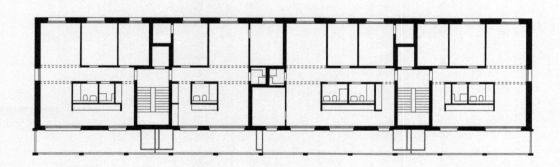

Biographies Marcus and Roger Diener

Marcus Diener

Born in 1918. 1934–1937 apprenticeship as a draughtsman in the office of Alban Werdenberg. 1939–1945 performed active service. 1942 Founding of the office Diener and Oberle, which he continued to run under the name of Marcus Diener Architect after Joseph Oberle's departure in 1950. Realized a large number of buildings, mainly around Basel. Built a large number of cooperative apartment buildings, later several cinemas, such as the Palace, Hollywood and Plaza, and urban residential and commercial buildings, including a complex with hotel and car silo based on the American model. Ran occasionally also an office in Toronto which built office buildings. Increasingly active as a developer. After 1960, large residential developments were built in Baselland. In 1980 hands over the management of his office to his son Roger Diener. Died in 1999.

Roger Diener

Born in 1950, 1970–1976 studied architecture at the ETH Zurich. Joined the office of his father Marcus Diener; since 1980 he has been managing the office of Diener & Diener Architects in Basel. Teaches at various schools of architecture, including Harvard University. 1987–1989 he is Professor of Design at the ETH Lausanne, 1999–2013 Professor at the ETH Zurich, headed the Studio Basel together with Jacques Herzog, Pierre de Meuron and Marcel Meili. Gives lectures on architectural questions, especially on the relationship to the built city. From 2005–2013 member of the Berlin Monuments Council, since 2013 member of the Federal Commission for Monument Preservation and since 2018 member of the Commission for Monument Preservation in Zurich. His buildings have received numerous prizes, he himself was awarded with the Grande Medaille d'Or of the Académie d'Architecture, Paris, in 2002, the Grand Prix Suisse d'art in 2010 and the Culture Prize of the City of Basel in 2019; in 2019 honorary doctor at the Bauhaus University Weimar.

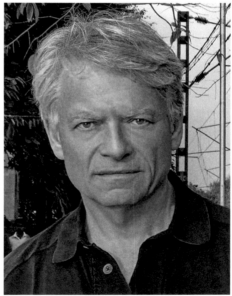

Biographies of the editors

Alexandre Aviolat

Born in 1985. 2004–2010 studied architecture at the ETH Lausanne and the TU Dresden (2006–2007). 2010–2013 worked as an architect in the office Dreier & Frenzel, then at the Laboratoire de Théorie et d'Histoire de l'Architecture LTH 2 at the ETH Lausanne under the direction of Bruno Marchand on a study on housing of the estates of Lausanne-West. Since 2014 research assistant within the research of the LTH 2, participation in various publications on housing. At the same time working as a partner in the office Aviolat Chaperon Escobar Architects in Fribourg, founded in 2014.

Bruno Marchand

Born in 1955. 1974–1980 studied architecture at the ETH Lausanne. Worked as an architect in the office of Lamunière, van Bogaert and at the same time doing research on the typology of housing in Geneva, leading to a PhD in 1992. 1996–2004 Executive Assistant at the Planning Department (SAT) of the Canton of Vaud. 1997–2020 Professor of architectural theory at the ETH Lausanne, head of the Laboratoire de Théorie et d'Histoire de l'Architecture LTH 2. Research on architecture and urban development in the 20th century and the present, and on Housing. Large number of publications in magazines and books, director of the *Cahiers de théorie and Matières* series. 2001–2014 Partner of Devanthéry Lamunière for urban development, since then freelance work in planning and urban development.

Martin Steinmann

Born in 1942. 1961–1967 studied architecture at the ETH Zurich. Worked as an architect in the office of Ernst Gisel, 1968–1978 assistant to Adolf Max Vogt and research assistant at the Institute for History and Theory of Architecture at the ETH Zurich, director of the CIAM Archives, 1978 doctorate on the Congrès Internationaux d'Architecture Moderne CIAM. Teaching at various schools of architecture, including the MIT and the ETH Zurich, 1975 curator of the exhibition "Tendenzen", 1980–1986 editor of the journal *Archithese*. 1987–2006 Professor of architectural design and architectural theory at ETH Lausanne, head of the Laboratoire de l'habitation urbaine. Publication of a large number of texts on 20th century and contemporary architecture. 2016 Grand Prix Suisse d'art. Various cooperation on projects with Diener & Diener.

Image Credits

Diener & Diener, Basel:
p. 10, 36 top and bottom, 38, 41 middle, 53, 56, 57, 60/61, 62, 64, 66, 72, 80, 92, 93, 151, 154, 162, 167, 173 top and bottom

Hans-Rudolf Disch, Basel:
p. 21

Roland Halbe, Stuttgart:
p. 94, 96

Archiv François Maurice, Geneva:
p. 43

César san Millán, Vitoria:
p. 99

Stefan Mueller, Berlin:
p. 11, 95

Christian Richters, Berlin:
Cover, p. 8, 12, 13, 15, 22, 28, 52, 63, 71, 88, 98, 100/101, 108, 109, 110, 114, 116/117, 118, 119, 122/123, 125, 126, 127, 128, 130/131, 132, 133, 134, 141, 142

Wim Ruigrok, Amsterdam:
p. 102

Martin Steinmann, Aarau:
p. 16, 17 right, 33 top and bottom, 34 top and bottom, 41 bottom, 42 middle and bottom, 44, 67, 68, 74, 75, 78/79, 90/91, 104, 105, 107, 112, 113, 144, 145, 148/149, 152, 153, 156, 157, 158, 160/161, 166, 170/171

Bernhard Strauss, Freiburg i. Br.:
p. 86, 107

Clément Vergély, Lyon:
p. 17 l, 164, 165

Christian Vogt, Basel / Copyright © 2020, ProLitteris, Zurich:
p. 87

Yohan Zerdoun, Freiburg i. Br.:
p. 14, 82, 83, 84, 137, 138/139, 140

Thanks to the collaborators of Diener & Diener Architects: Dieter Righetti, Annina von Planta, Isabel Halene, Ralph Franz, Stephan Gude, Asa Norman Schneider, Guilherme Pires.

Thanks also to Frédéric Frank, Bärbel Gysi, Aline Lemmer and Christine Marchand.

Concept: Martin Steinmann, Bruno Marchand, Alexandre Aviolat
Project texts: Martin Steinmann
Project plans: Alexandre Aviolat
Translations: Bronwen Saunders, Basel (essays and conversation); Ian Pepper, Berlin (projects)
Proofreading: Christen A. Jamar, London
Design: Anne Hoffmann Graphic Design, Zurich, Anne Hoffmann, Jörg Schwertfeger
Lithography, printing, and binding: DZA Druckerei zu Altenburg GmbH, Thuringia

Cover image: Île Seguin, Apartment Building with Day Care Center, Boulogne-Billancourt, France, 2005–2009
Photo: Christian Richters

© 2020 Park Books AG, Zurich

© for the texts: the authors
© for the images: see image credits

Park Books
Niederdorfstrasse 54
8001 Zurich
Switzerland
www.park-books.com

Park Books is being supported by the Federal Office of Culture with a general subsidy for the years 2016–2020.

All rights reserved; no part of this publication may be reproduced, stored in a retrieval system or transmitted in any form or by any means, electronic, mechanical, photocopying, recording, or otherwise, without the prior written consent of the publisher.

ISBN 978-3-03860-185-2